Solace Suns

∞calm ∞ soothe ∞ cheer ∞ comfort ∞

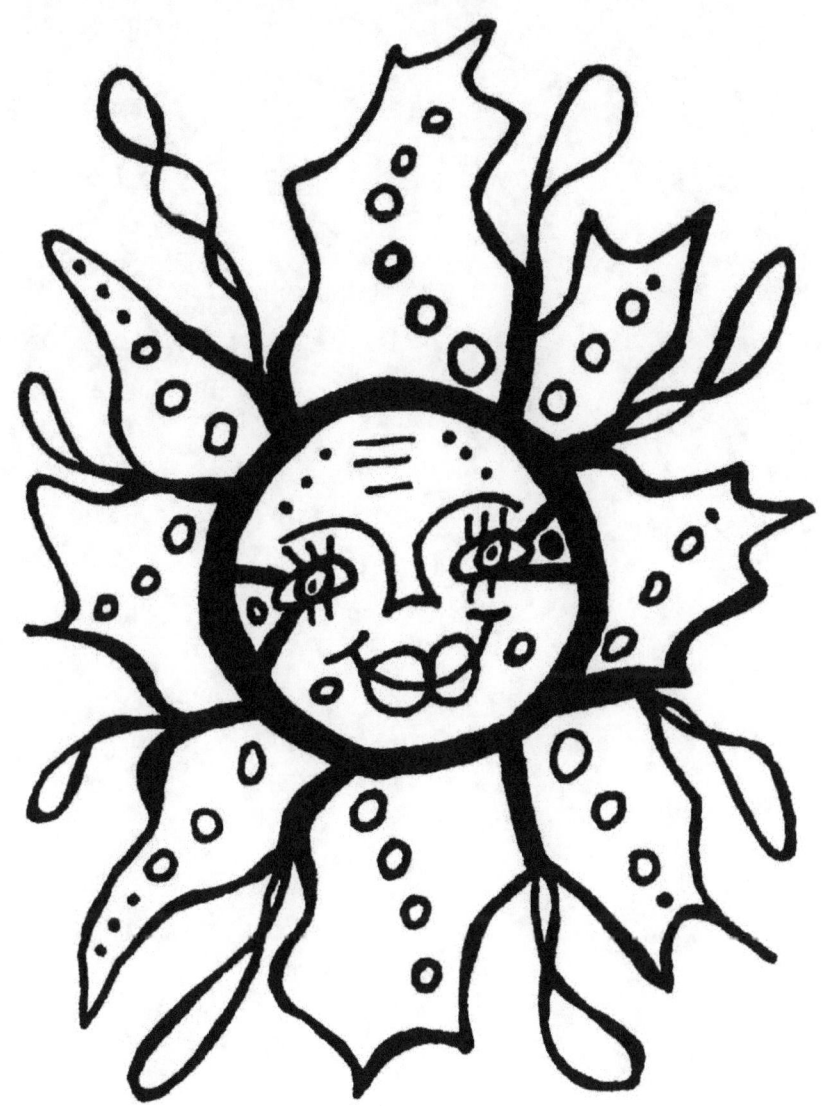

"A Larger Design Coloring Book"

Jenny Carlisle Carrington

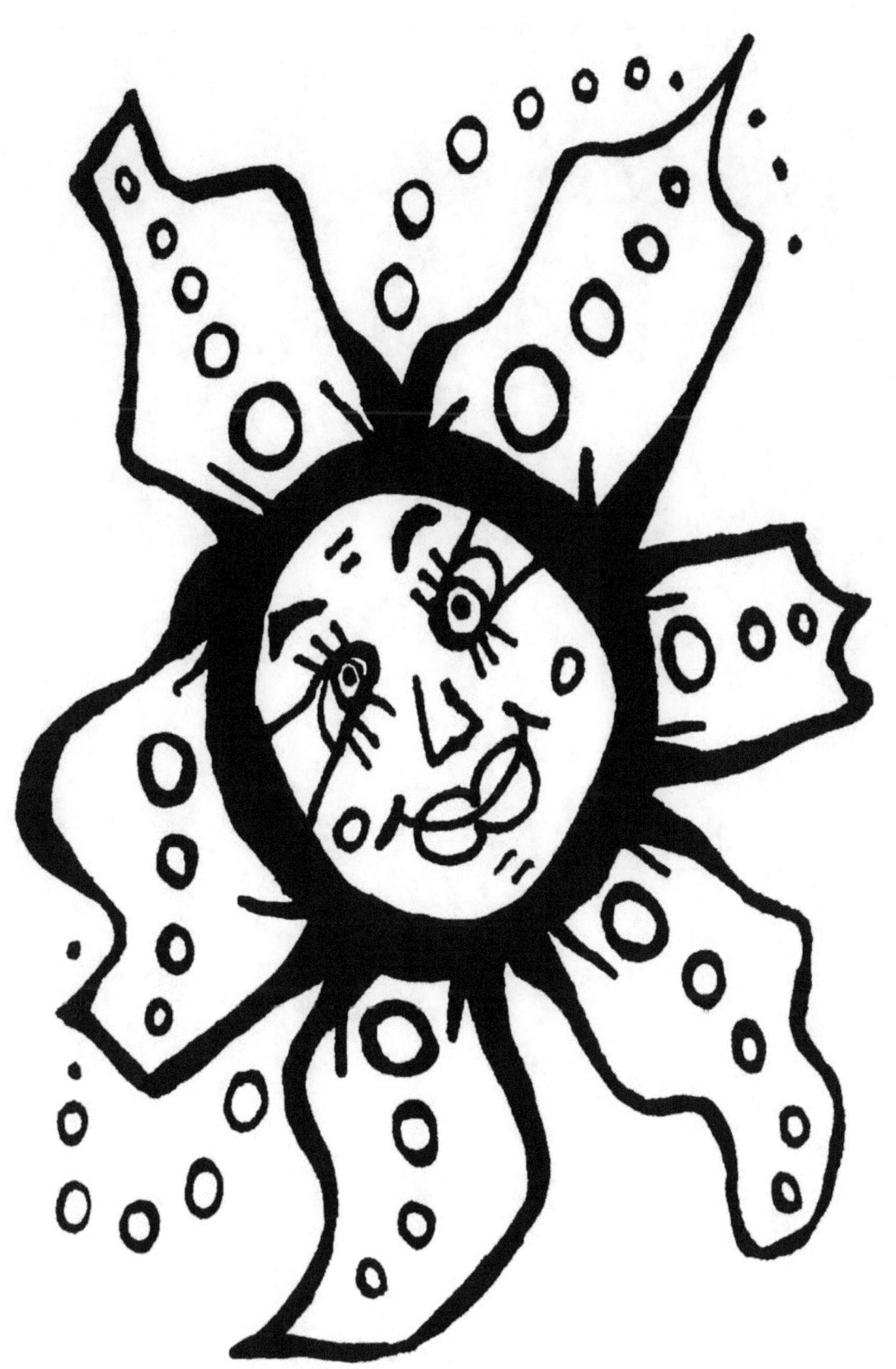

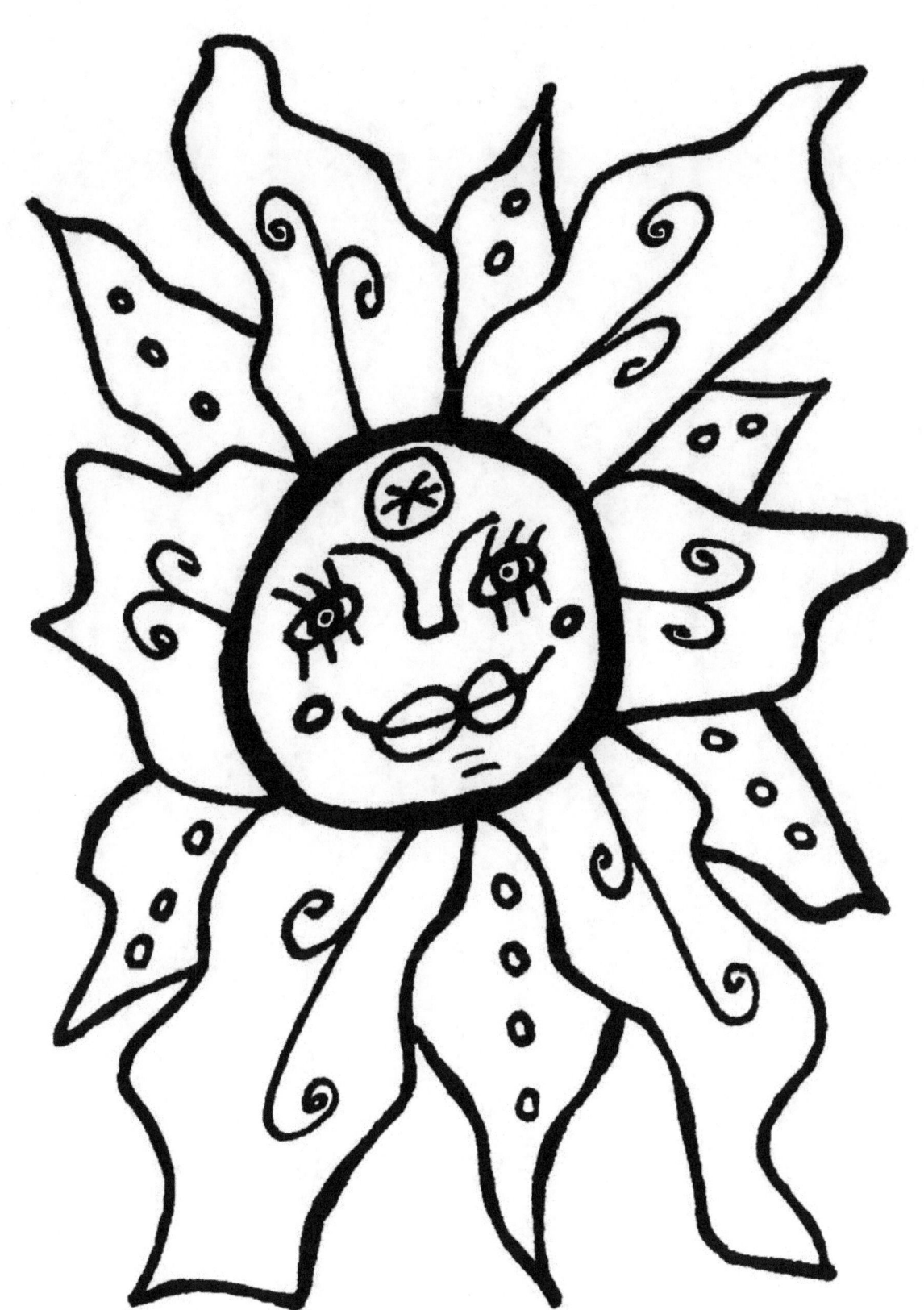

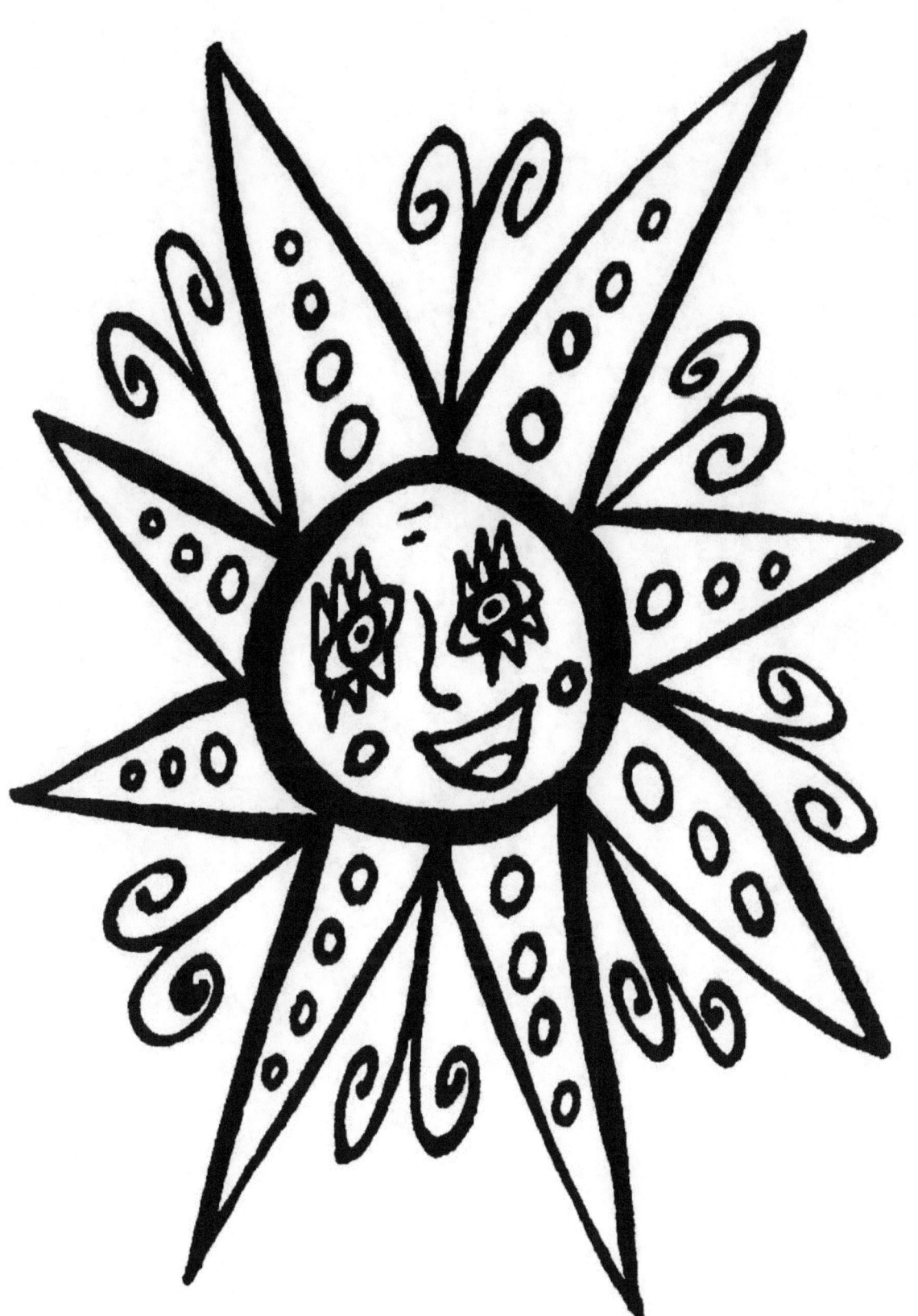

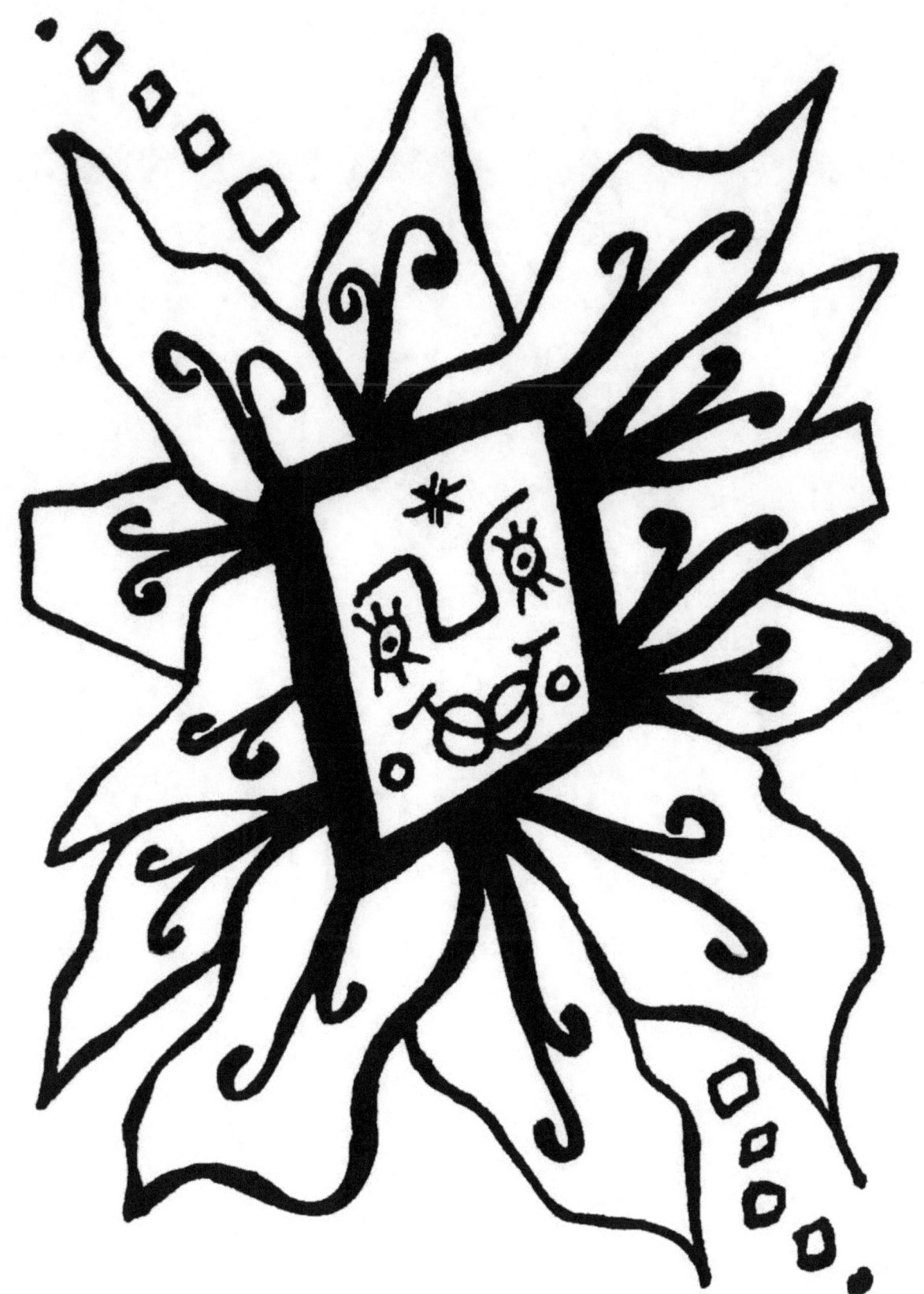

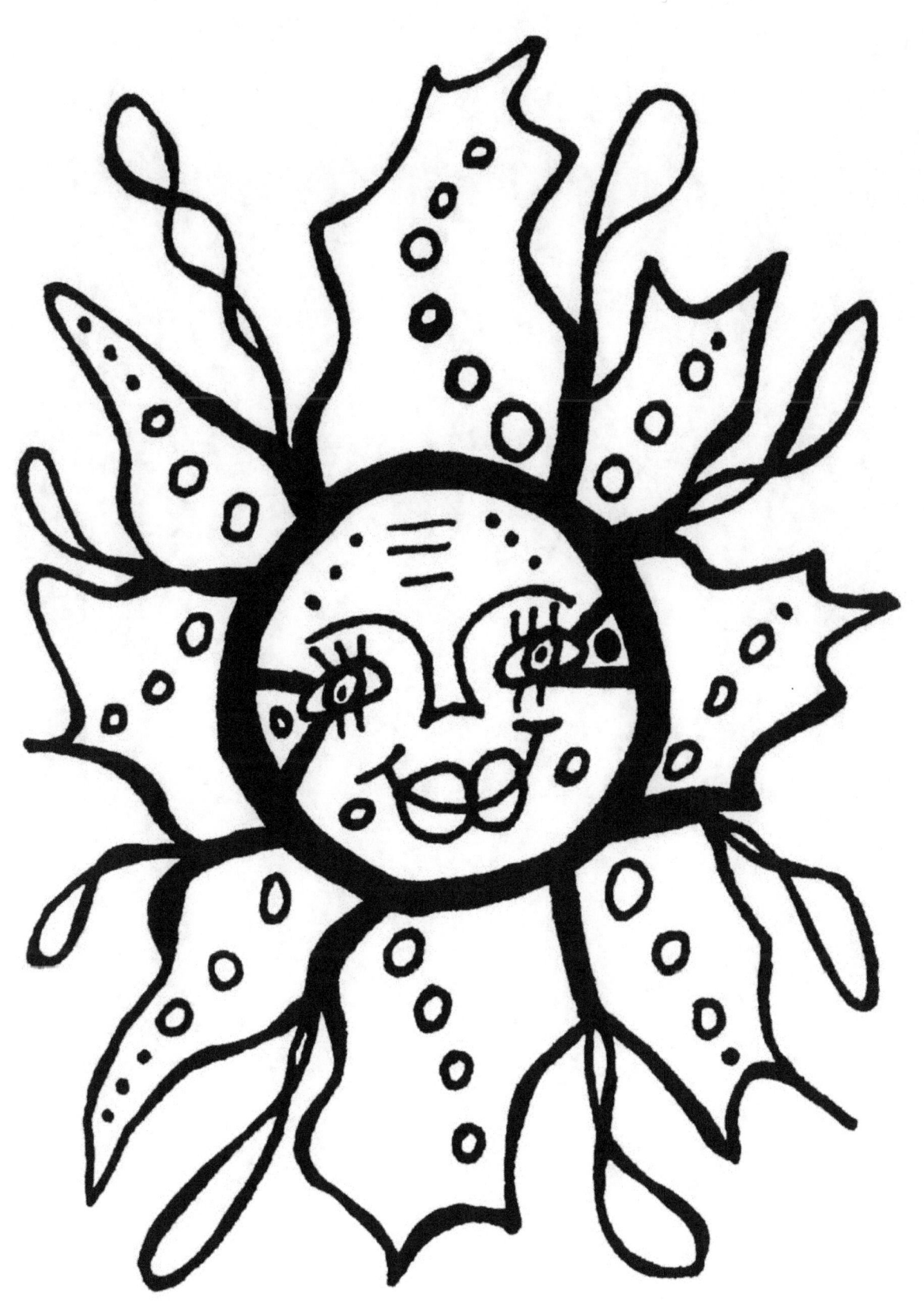

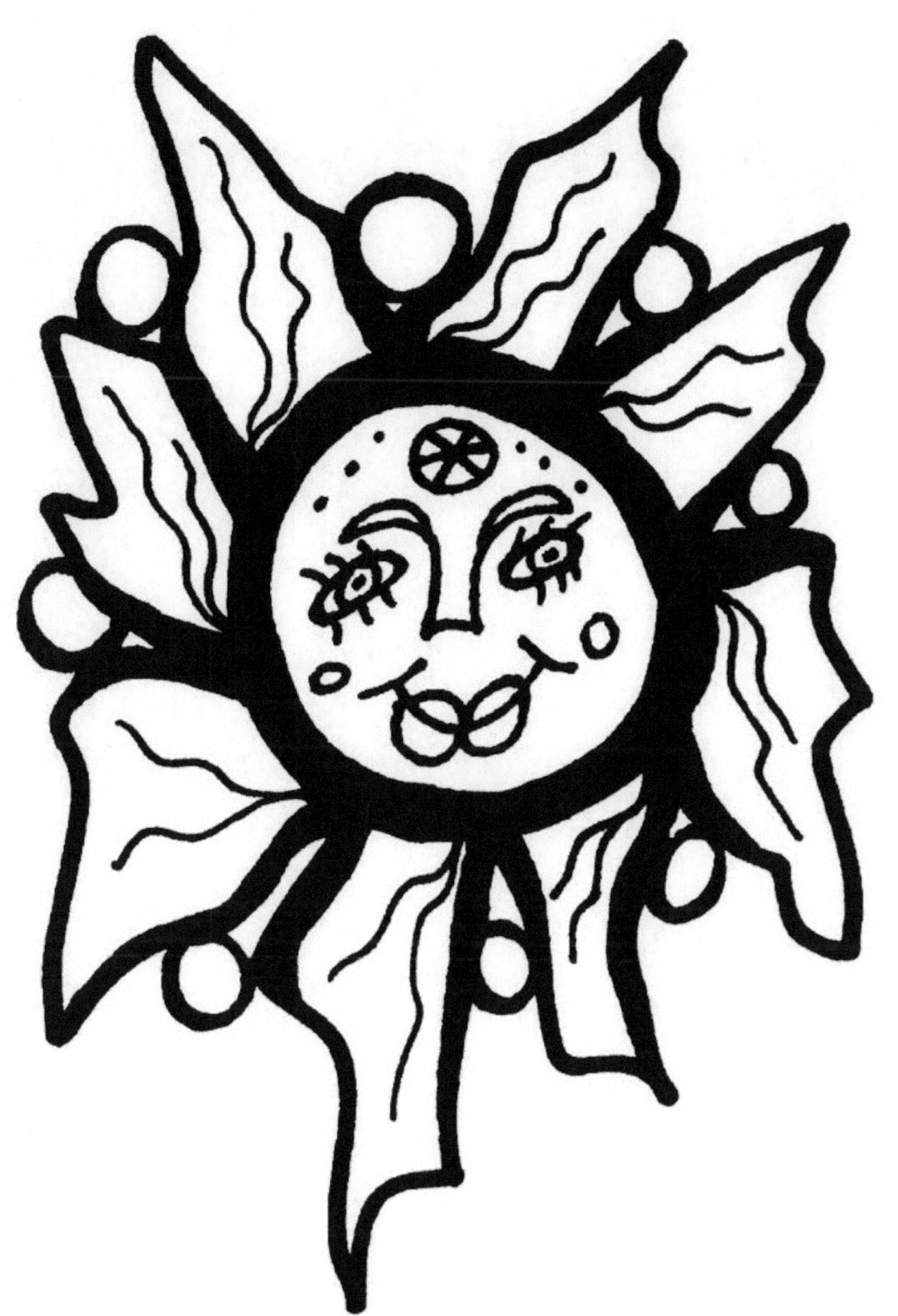

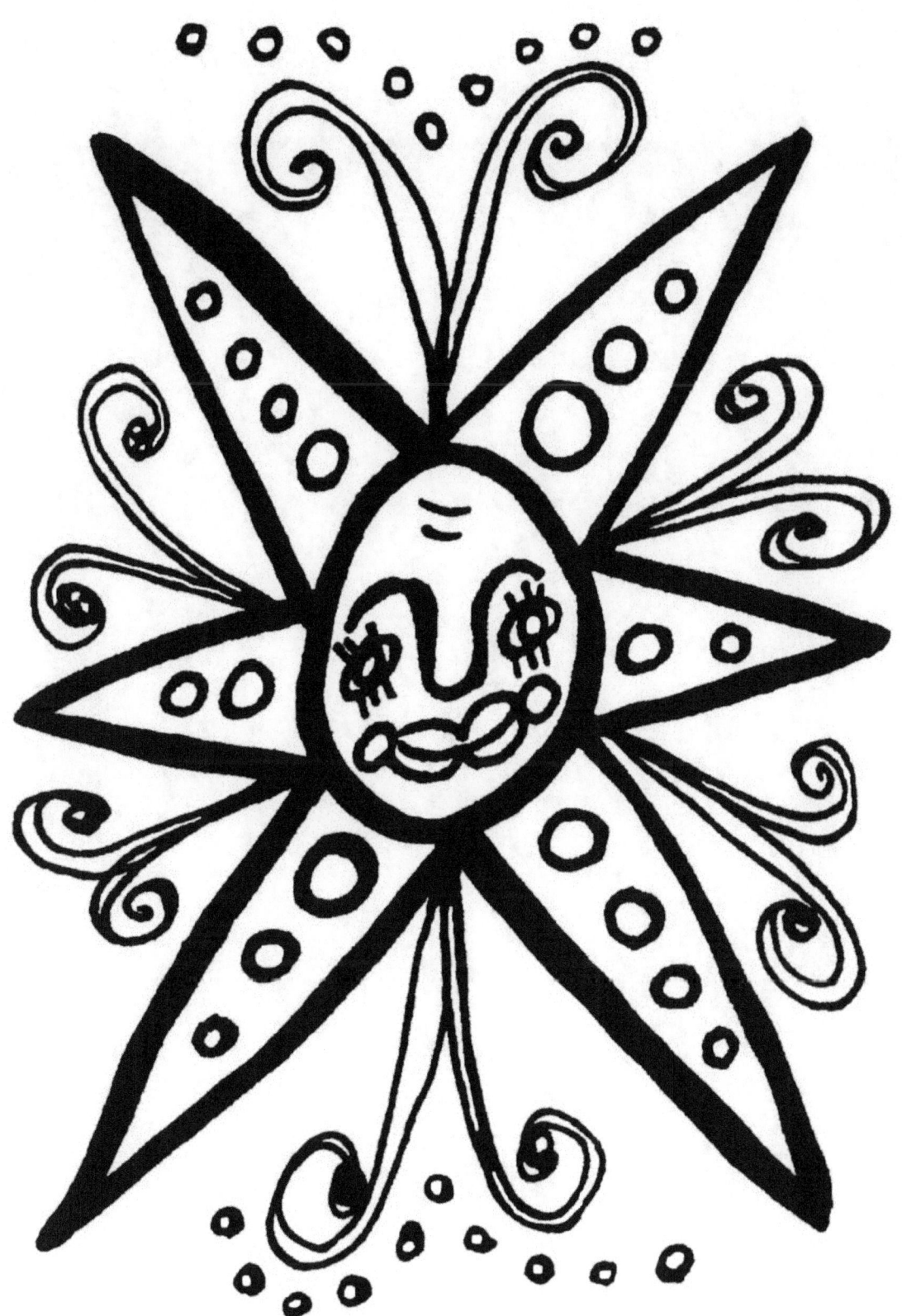

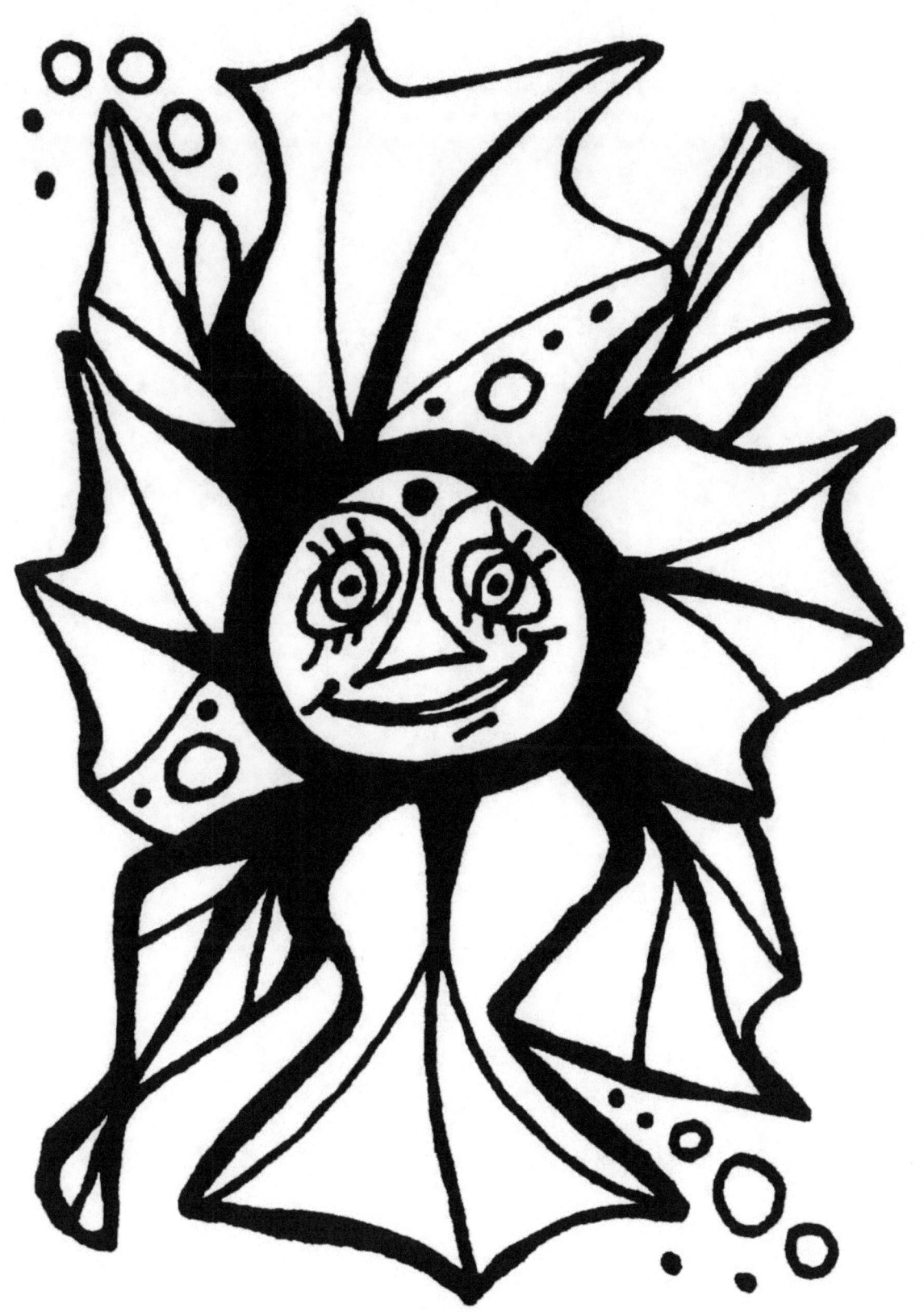

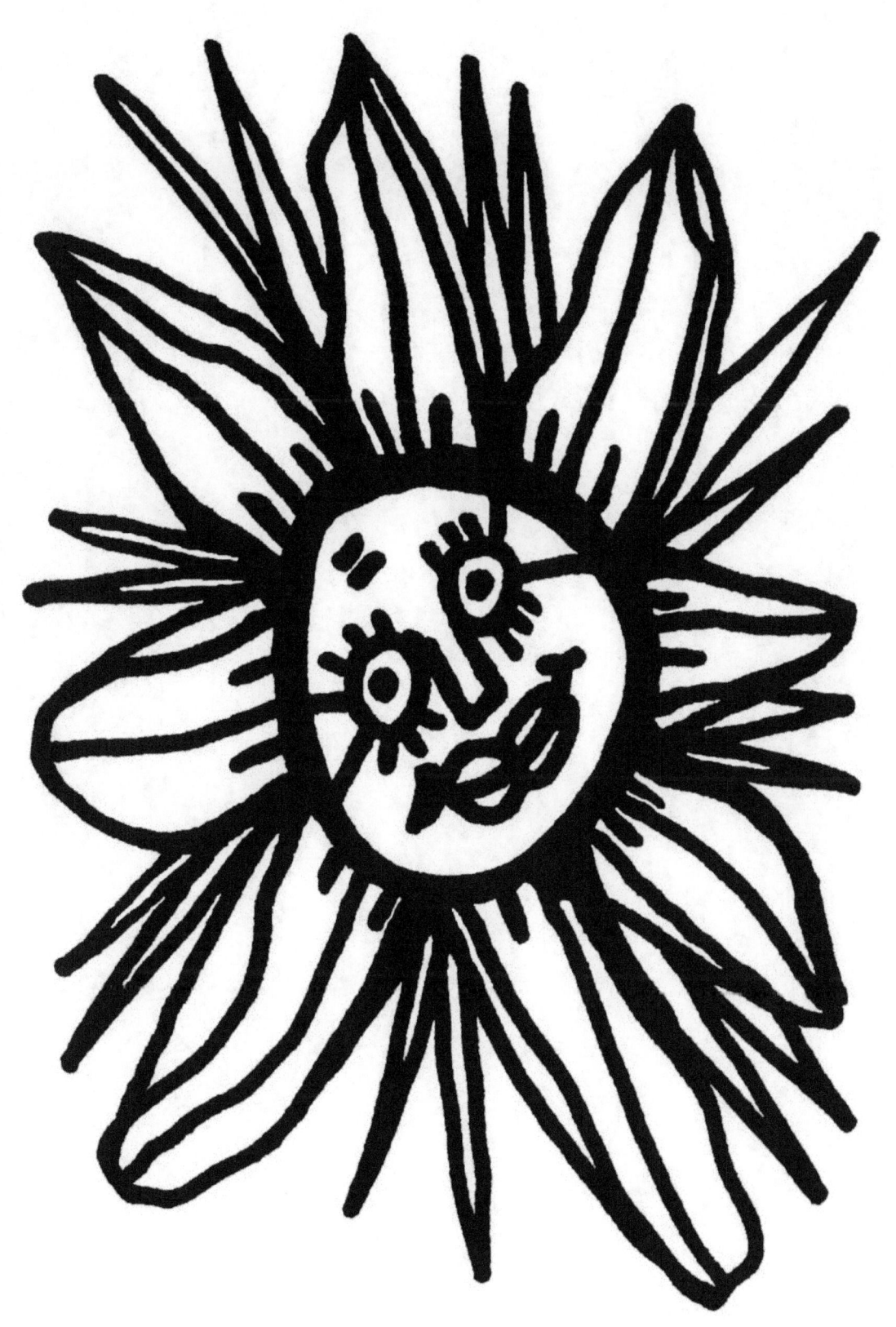

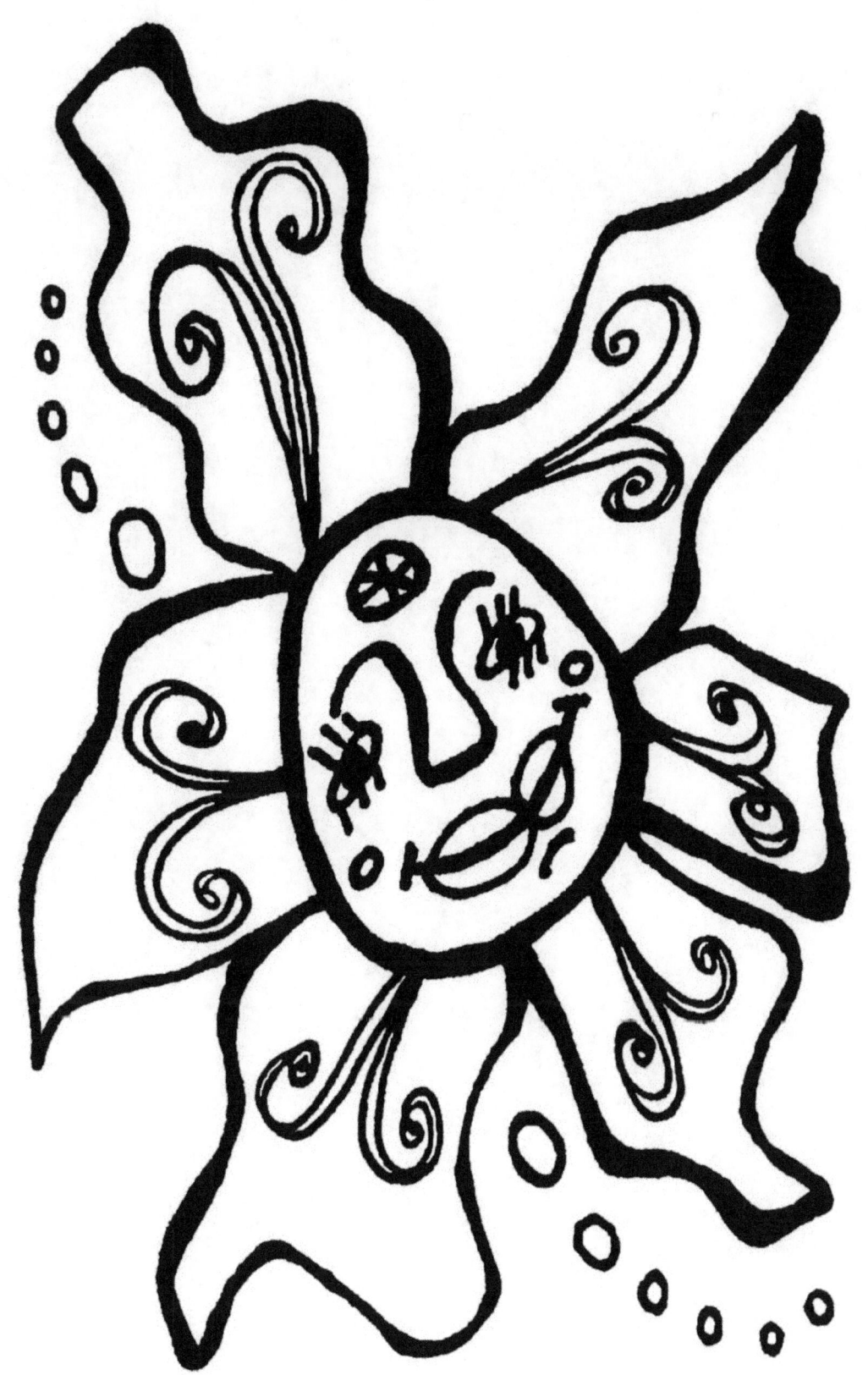

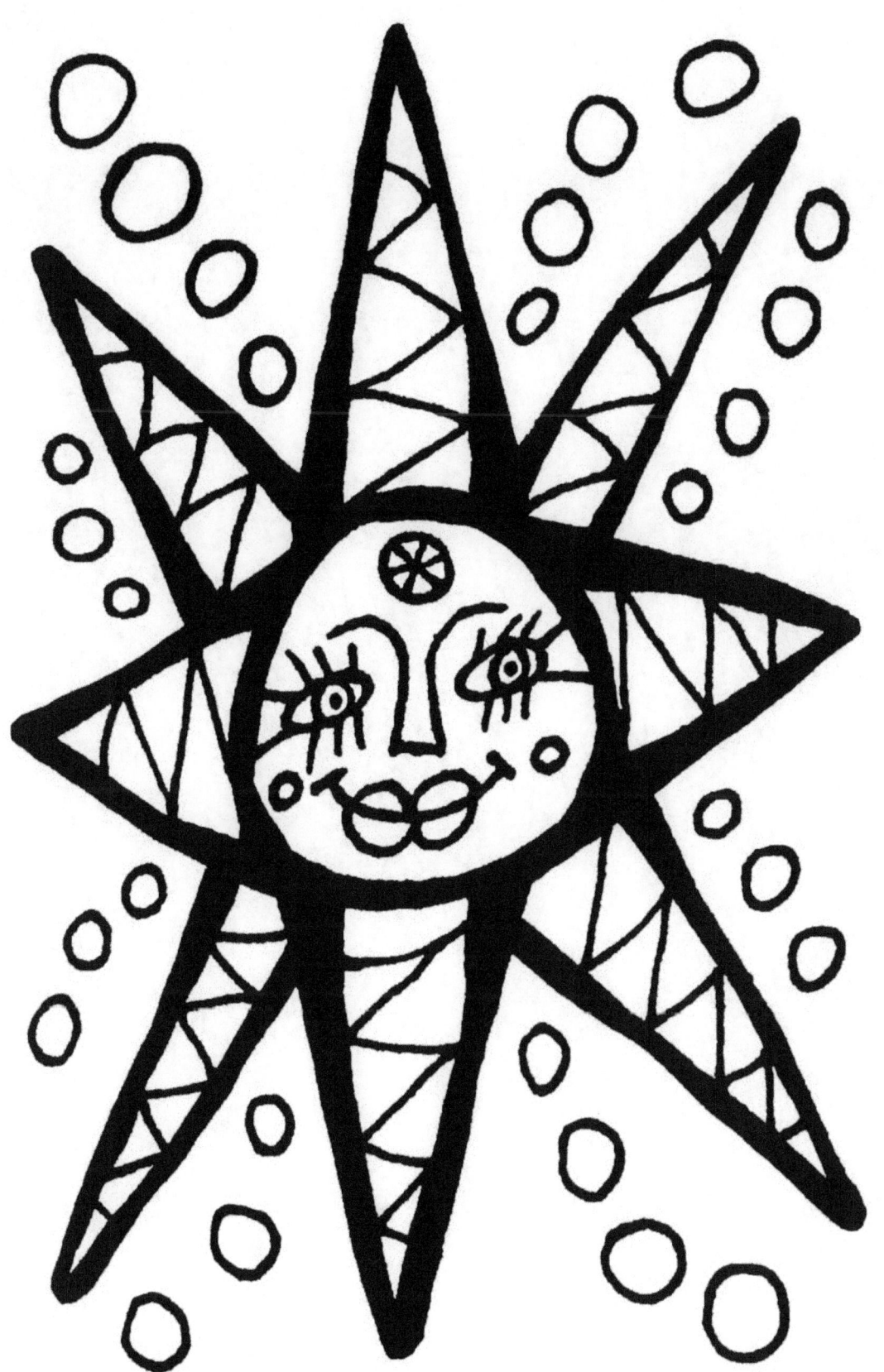

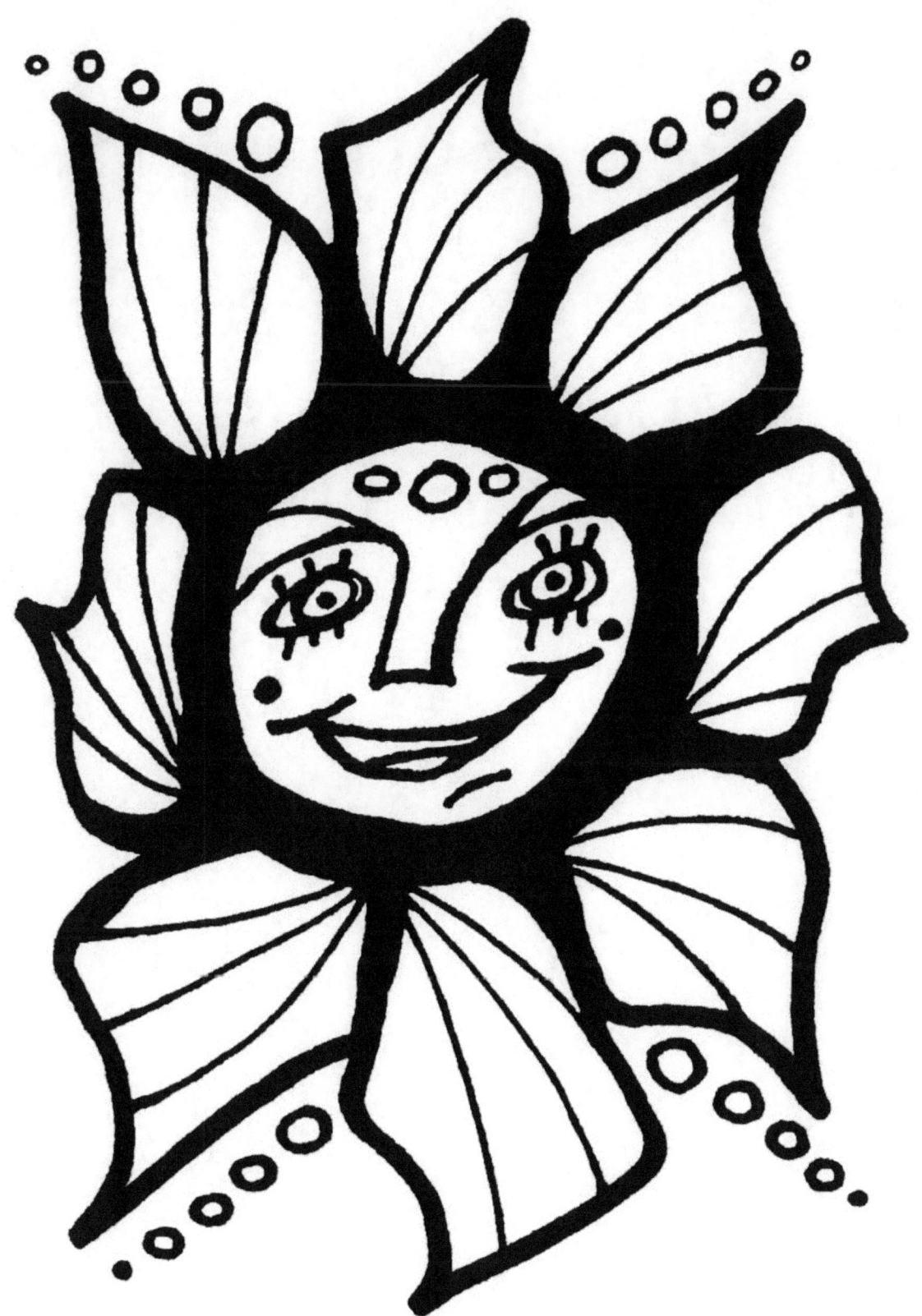

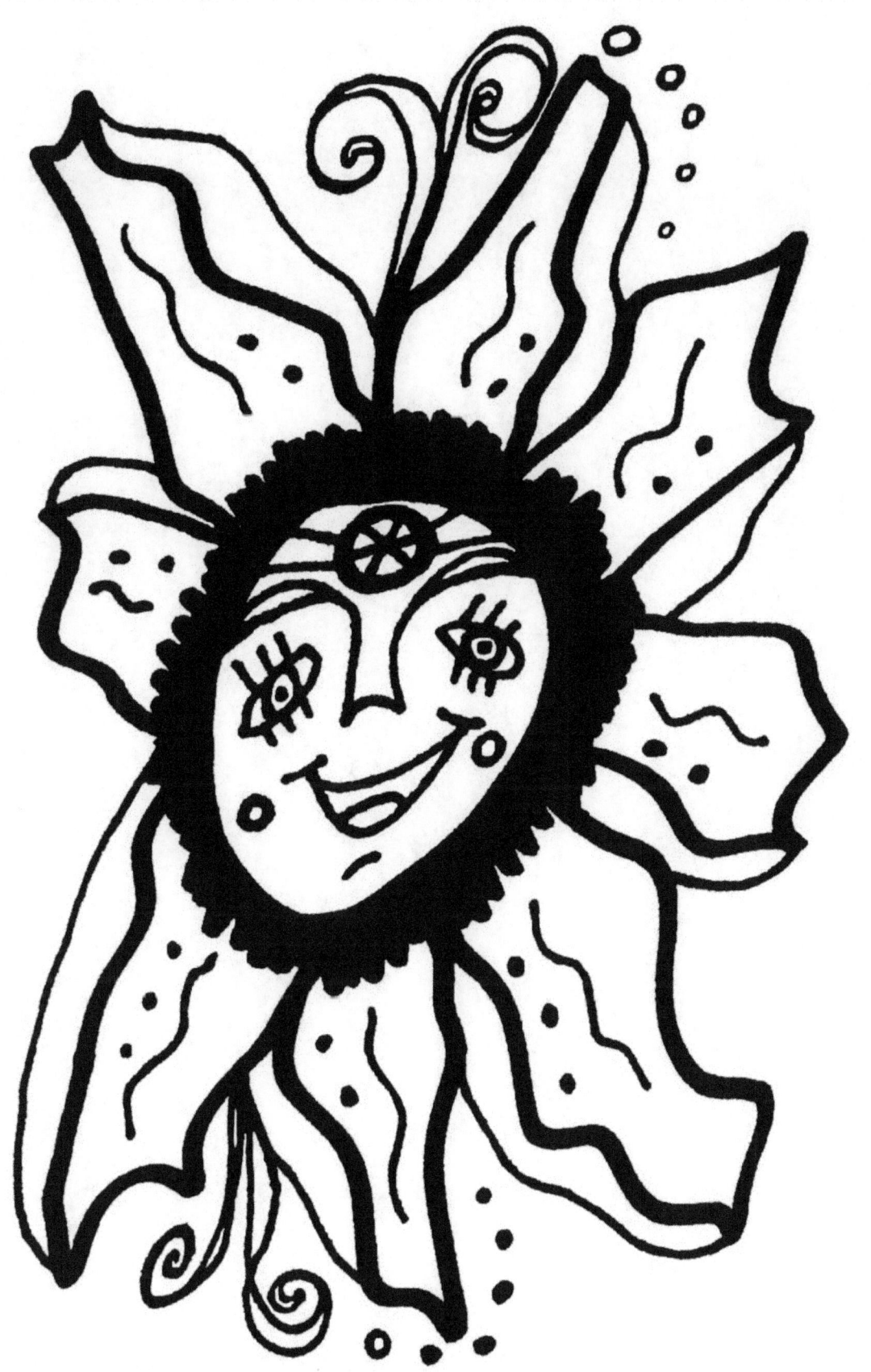

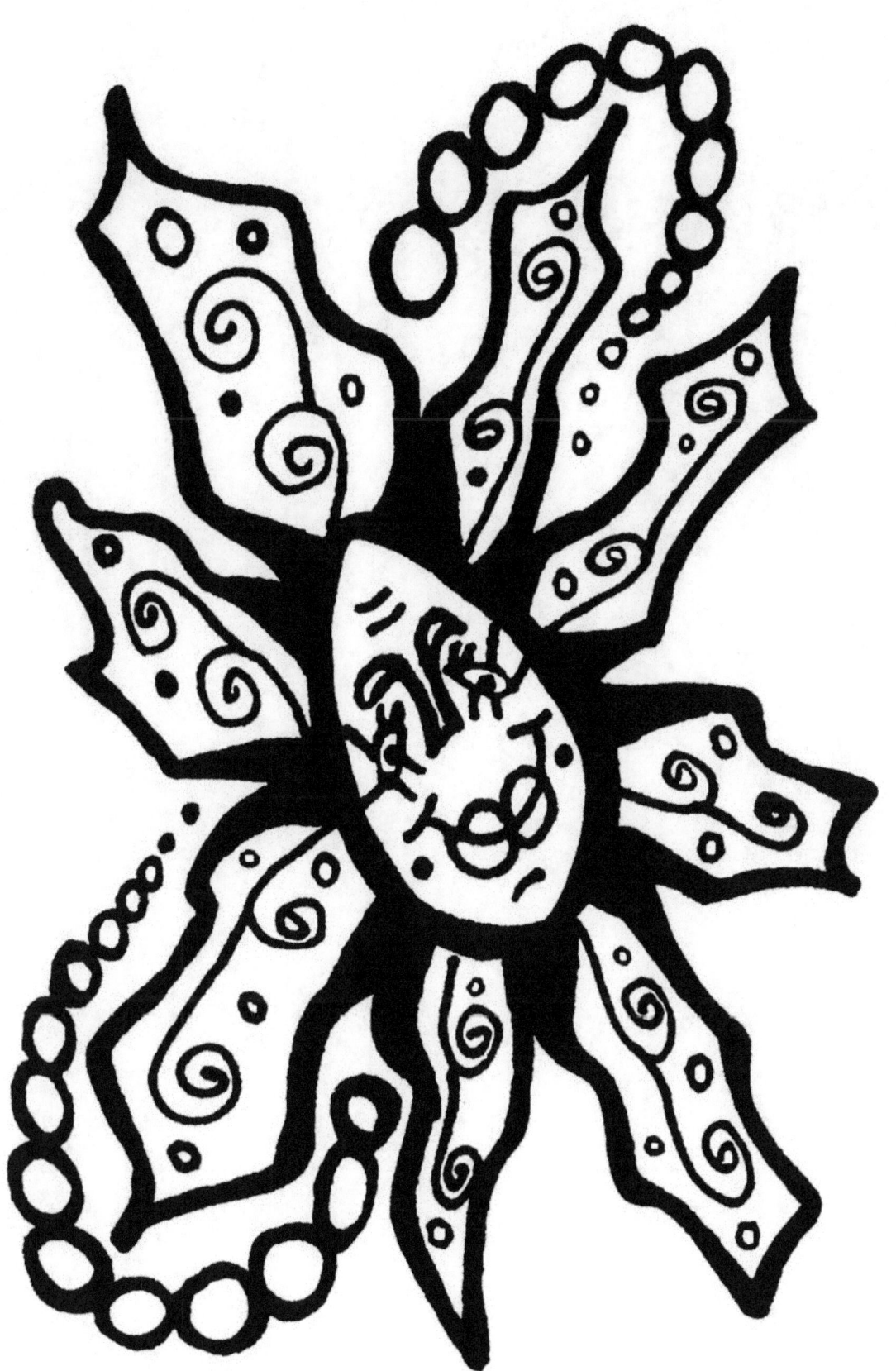

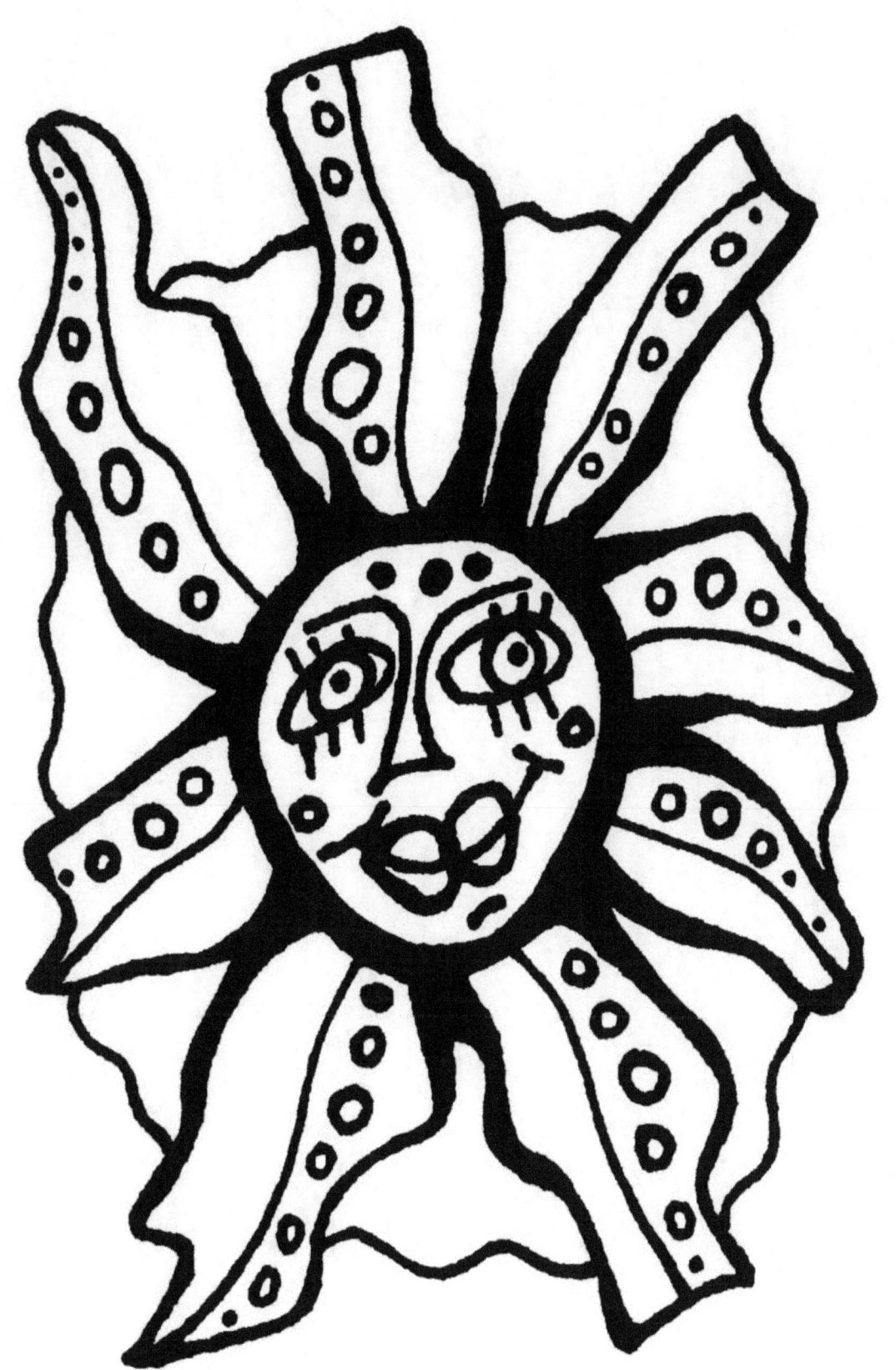

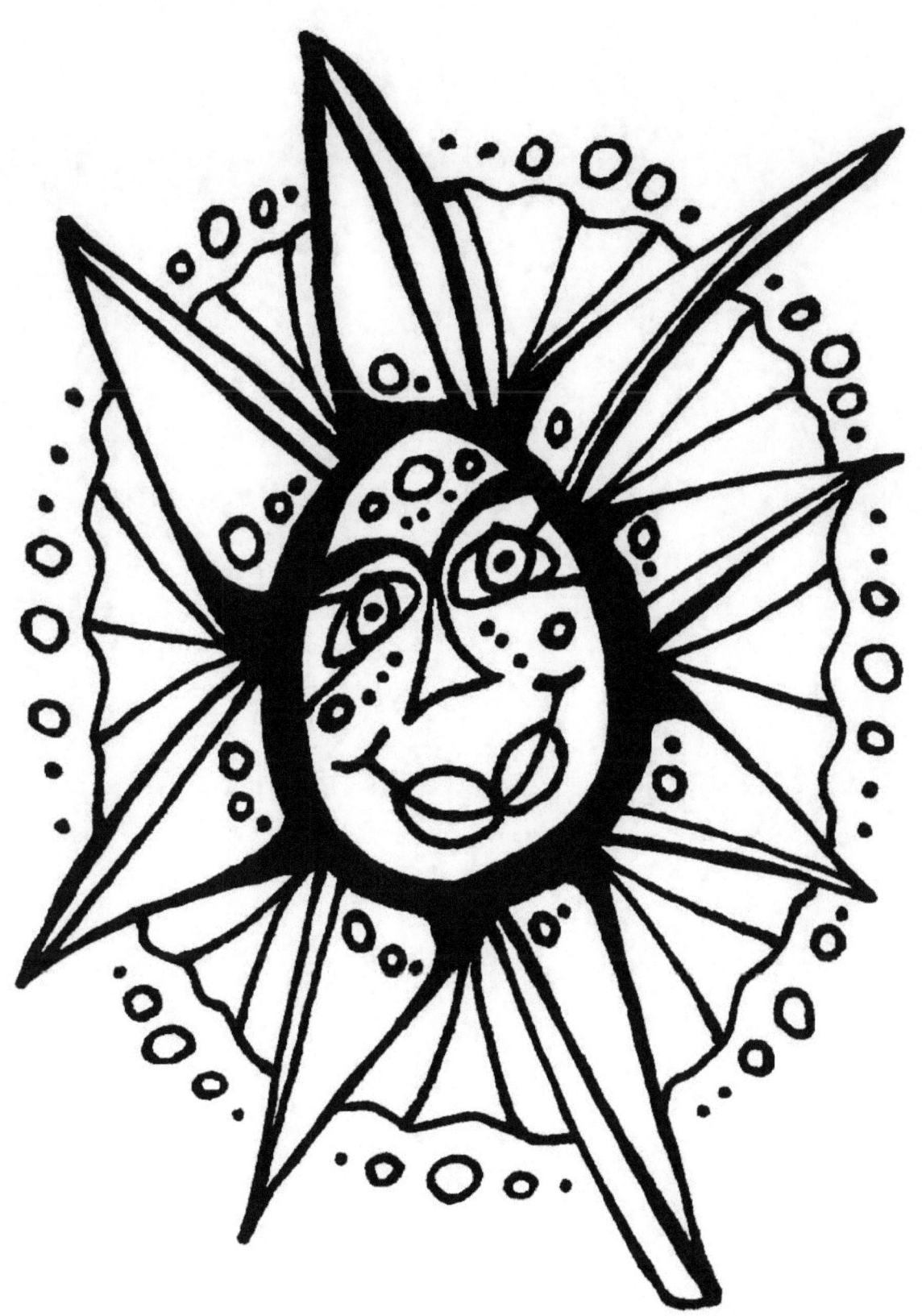

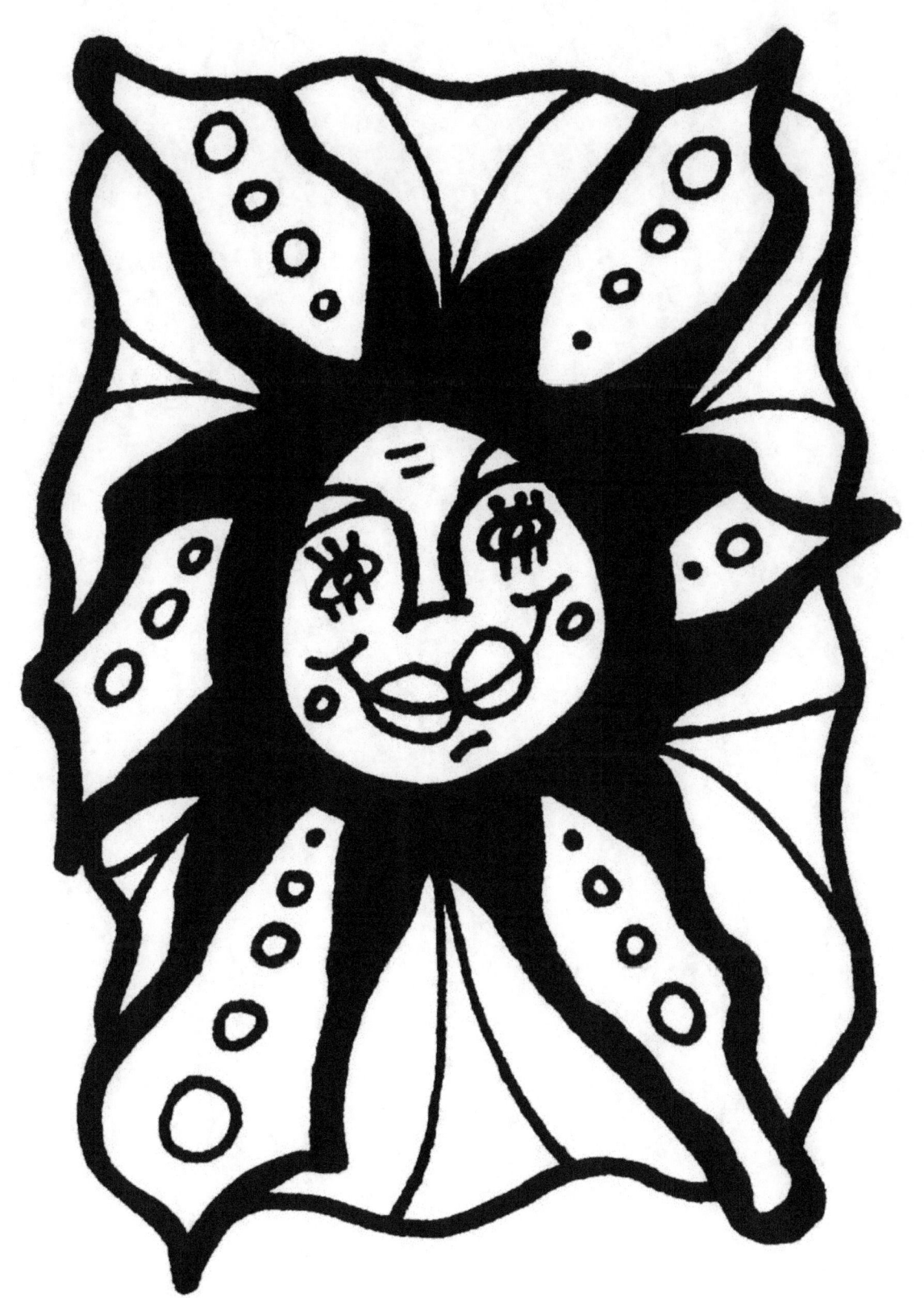

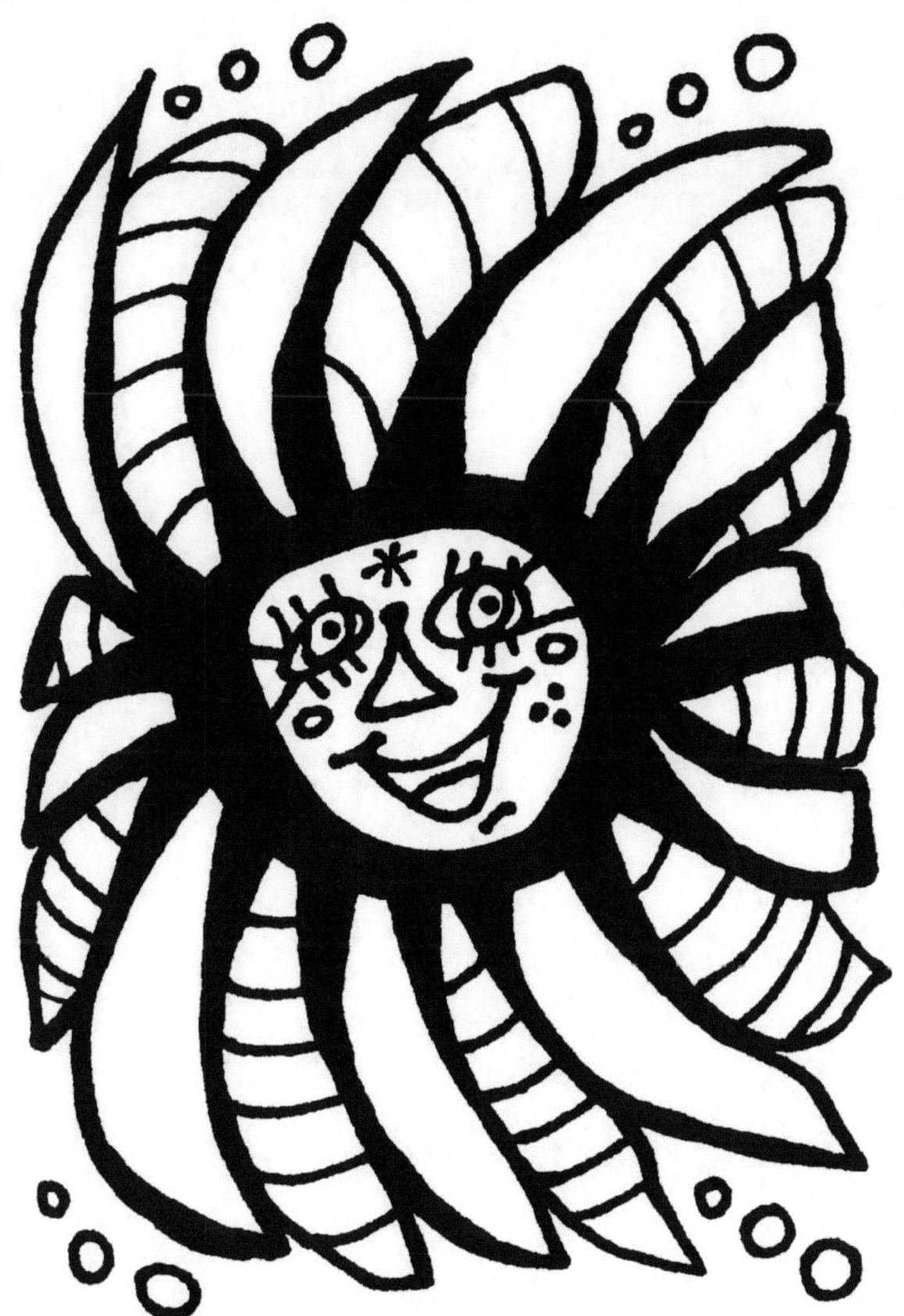

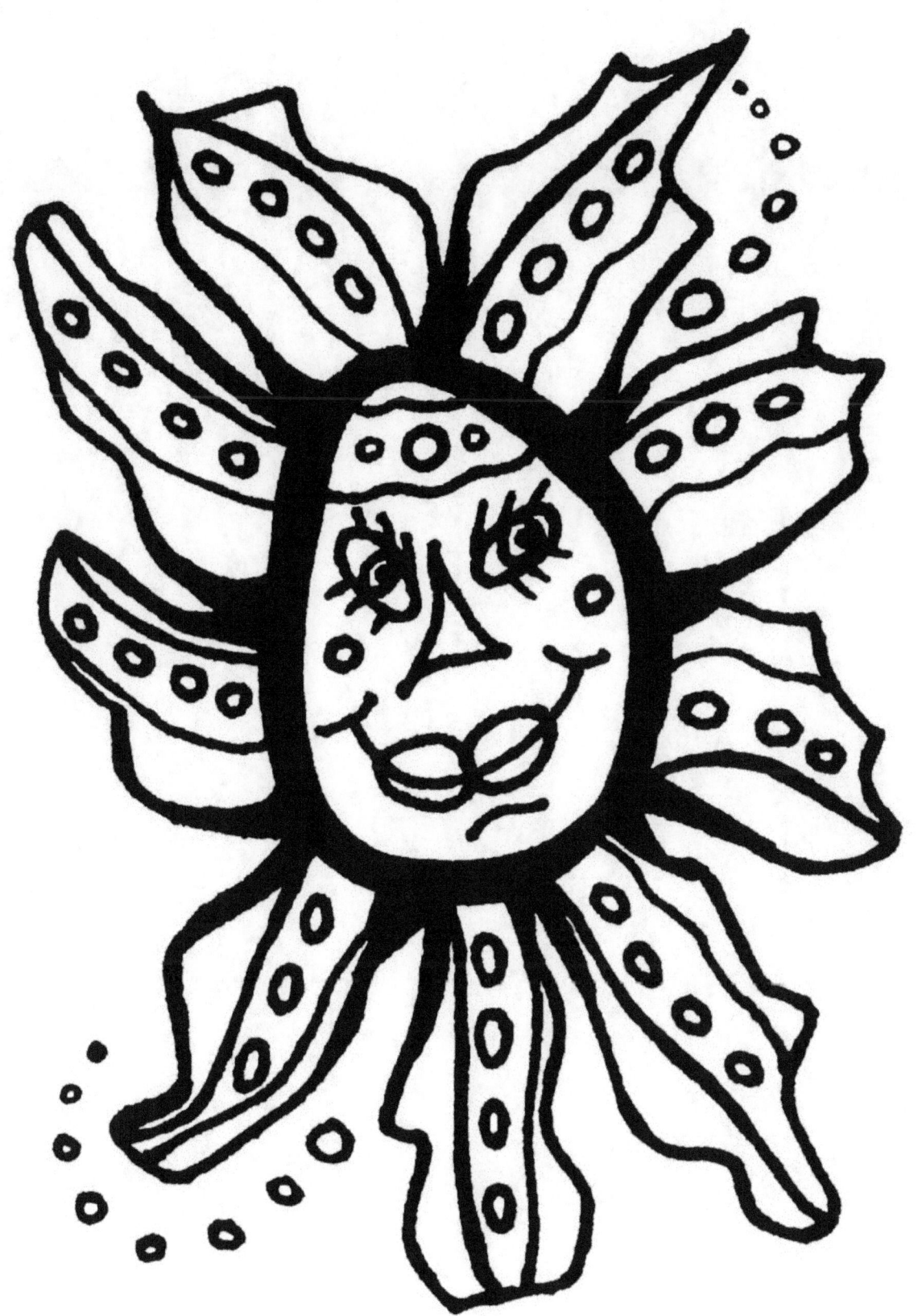

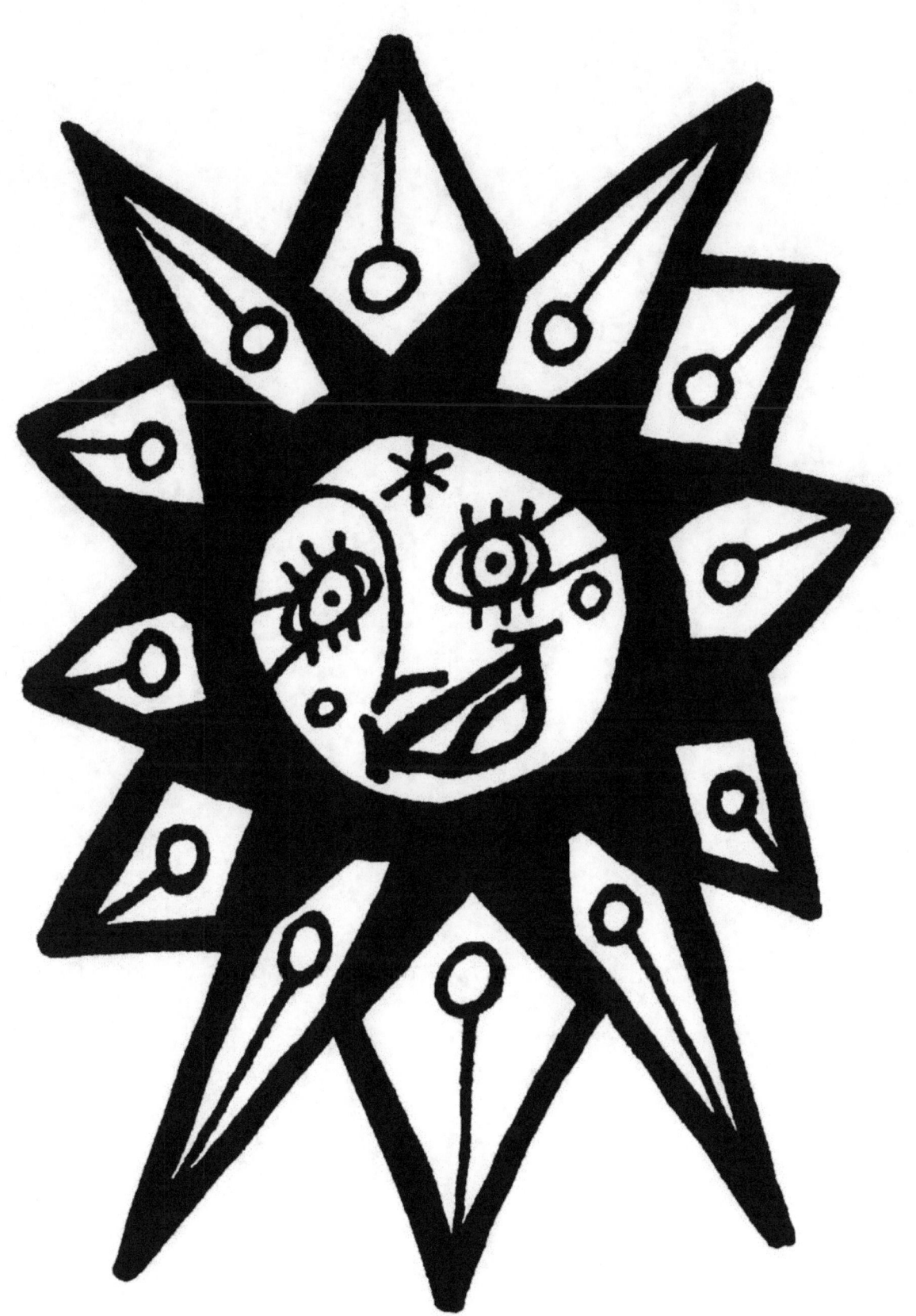

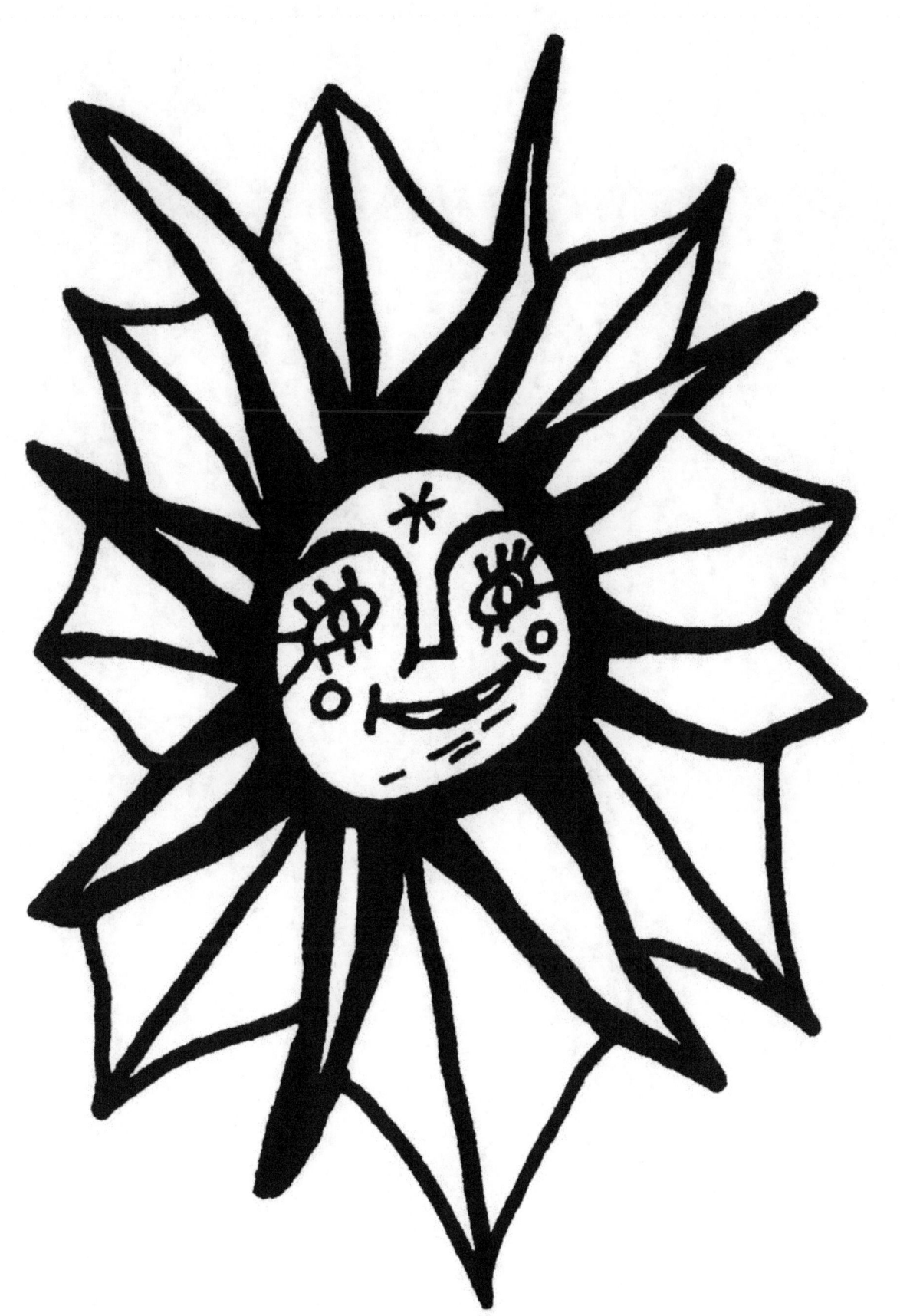

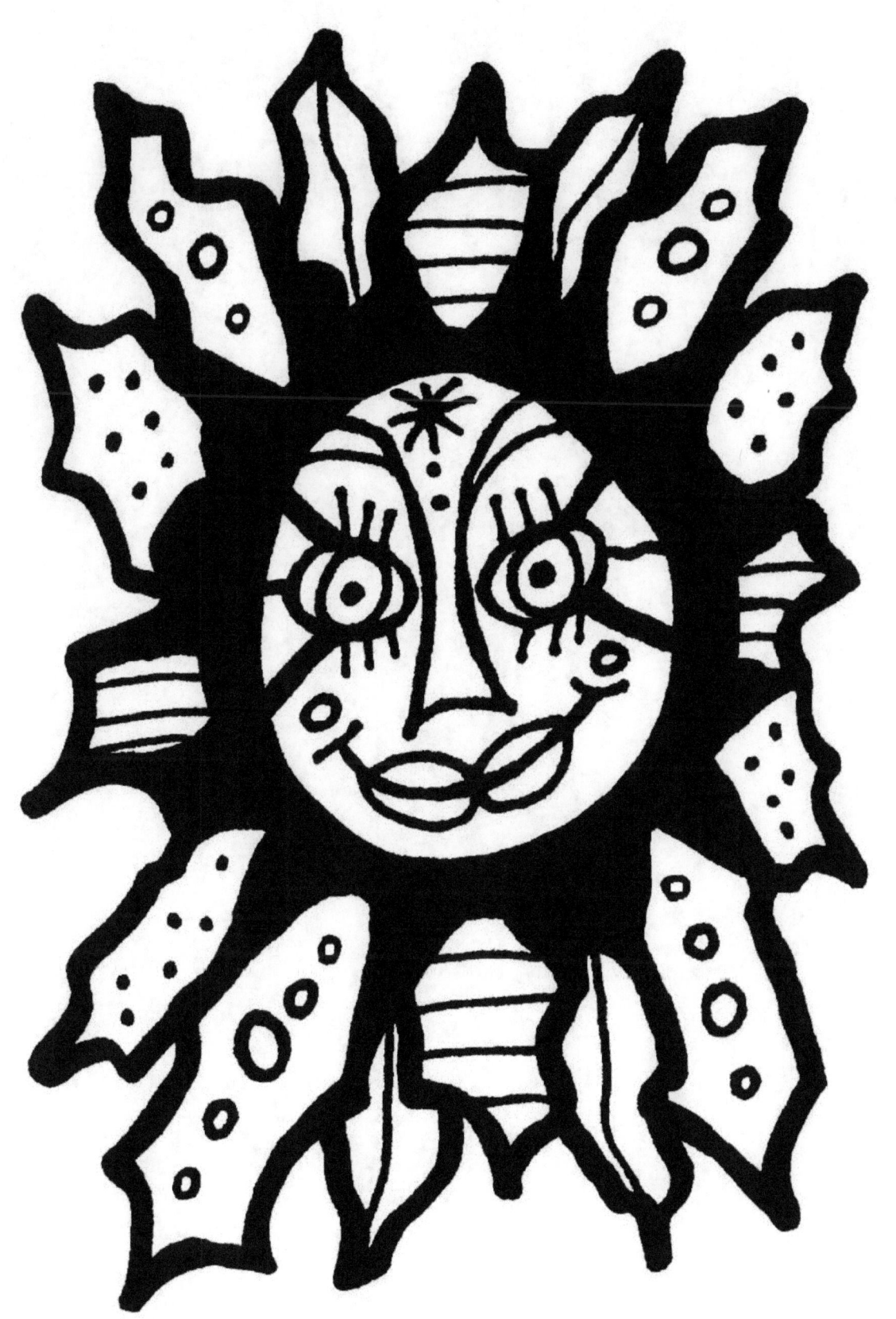

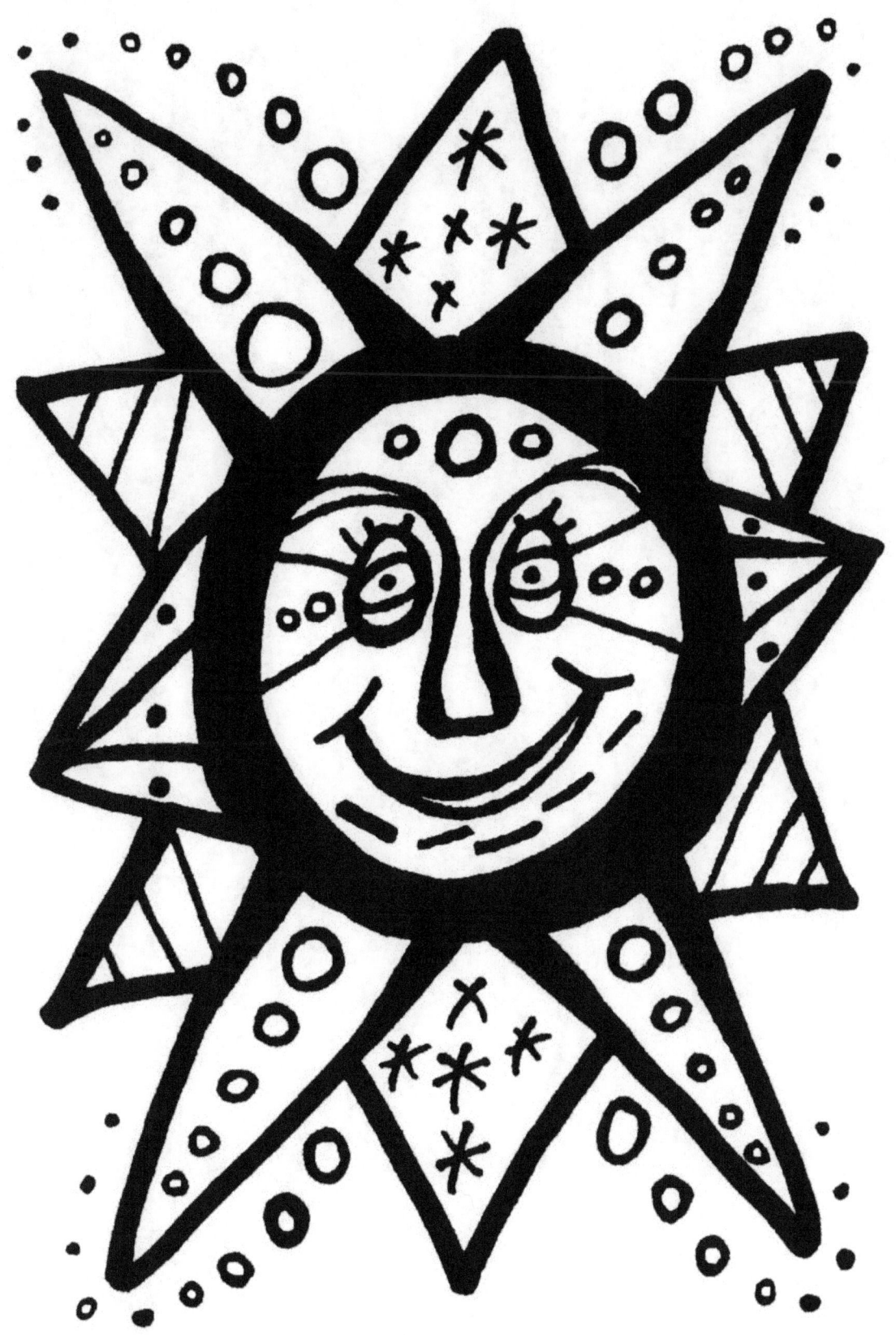

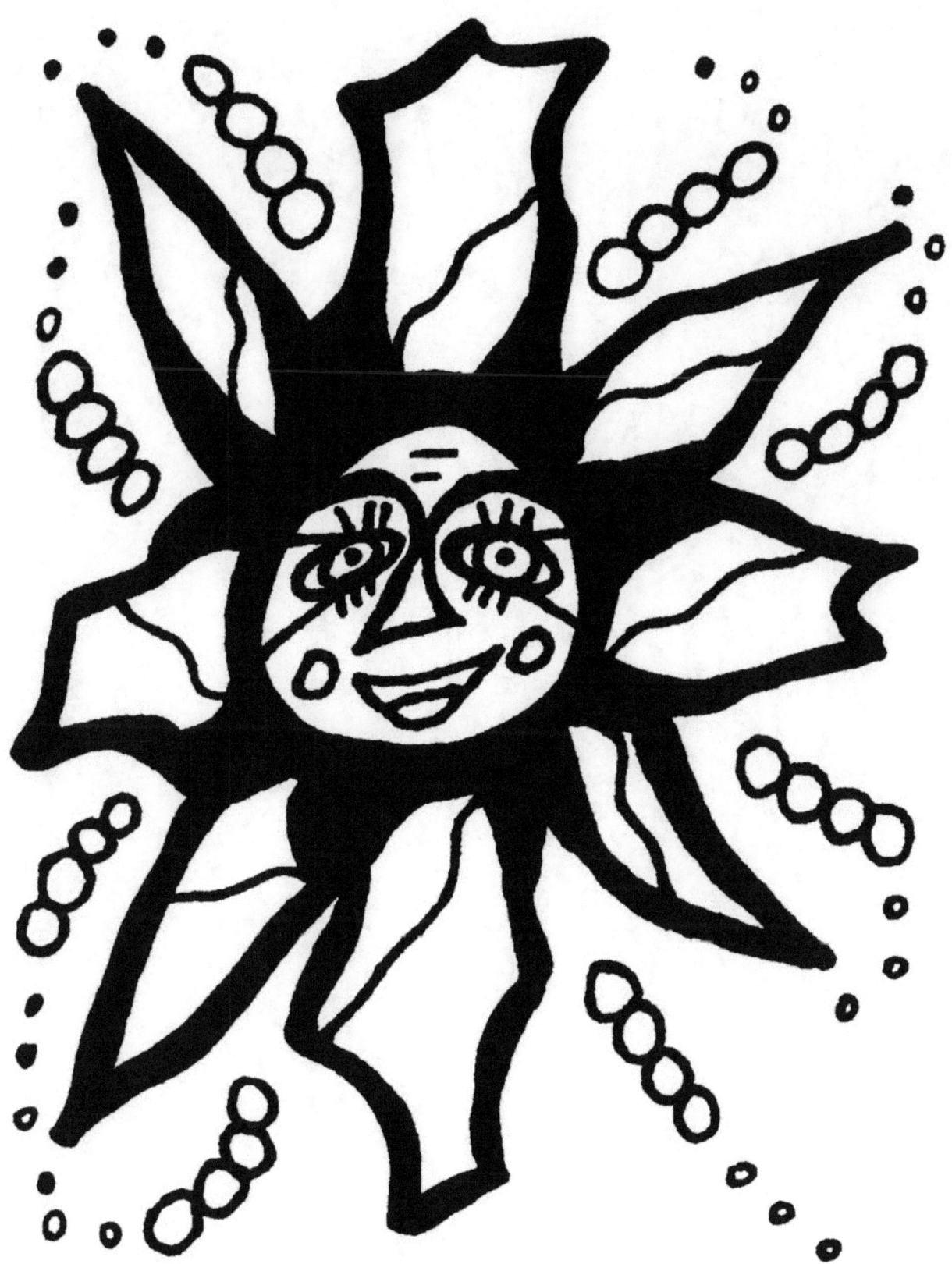

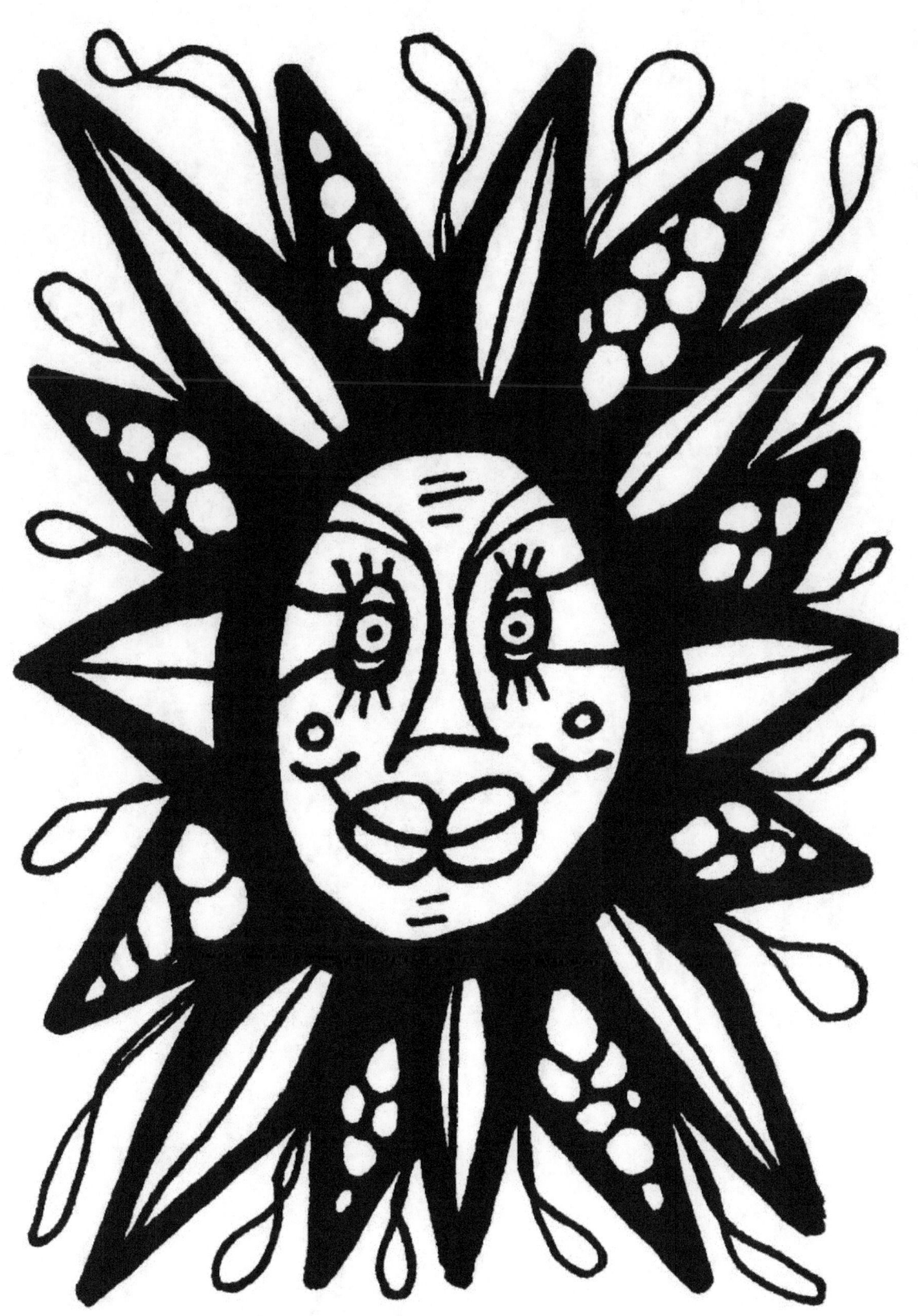

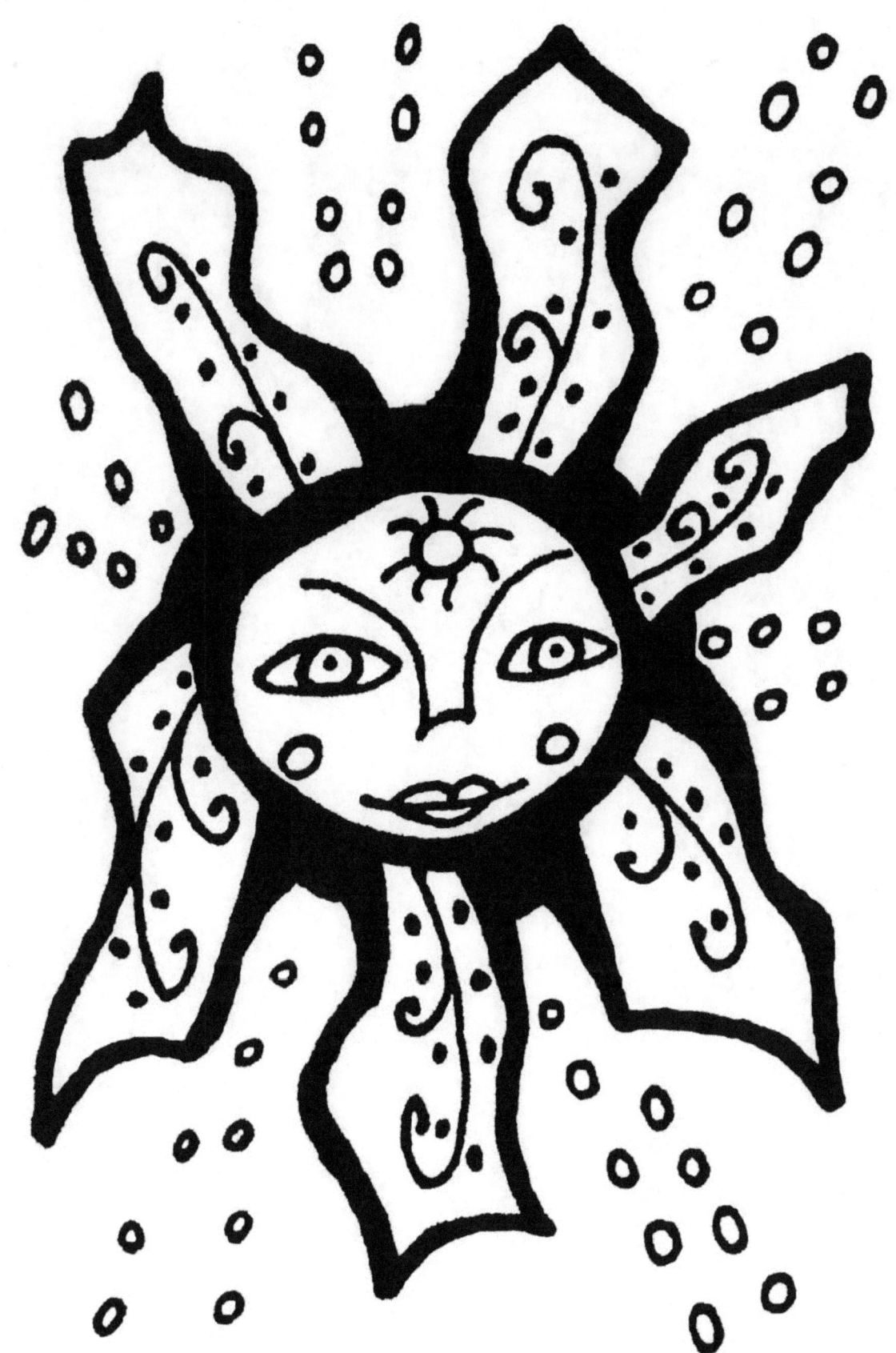

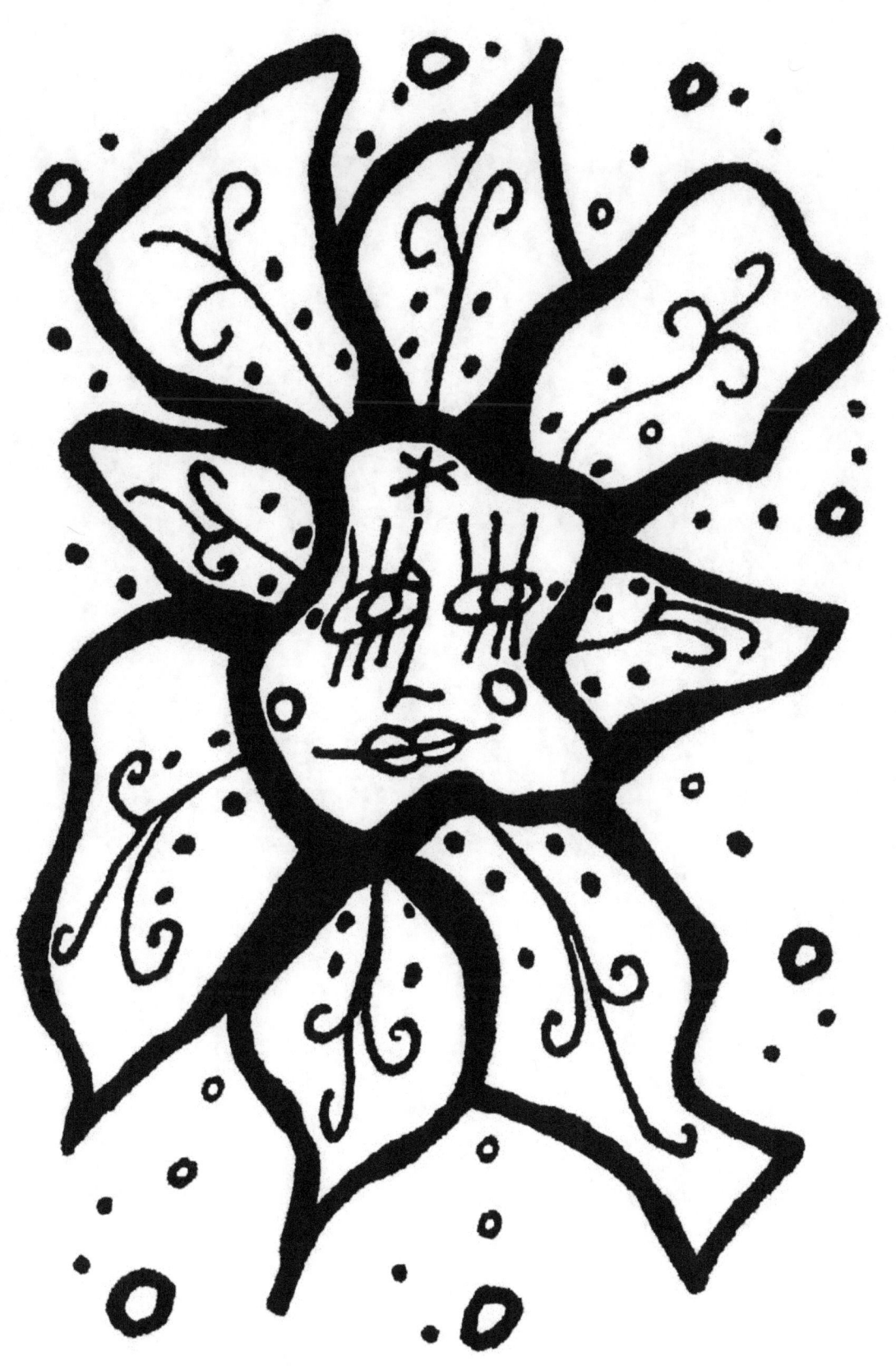

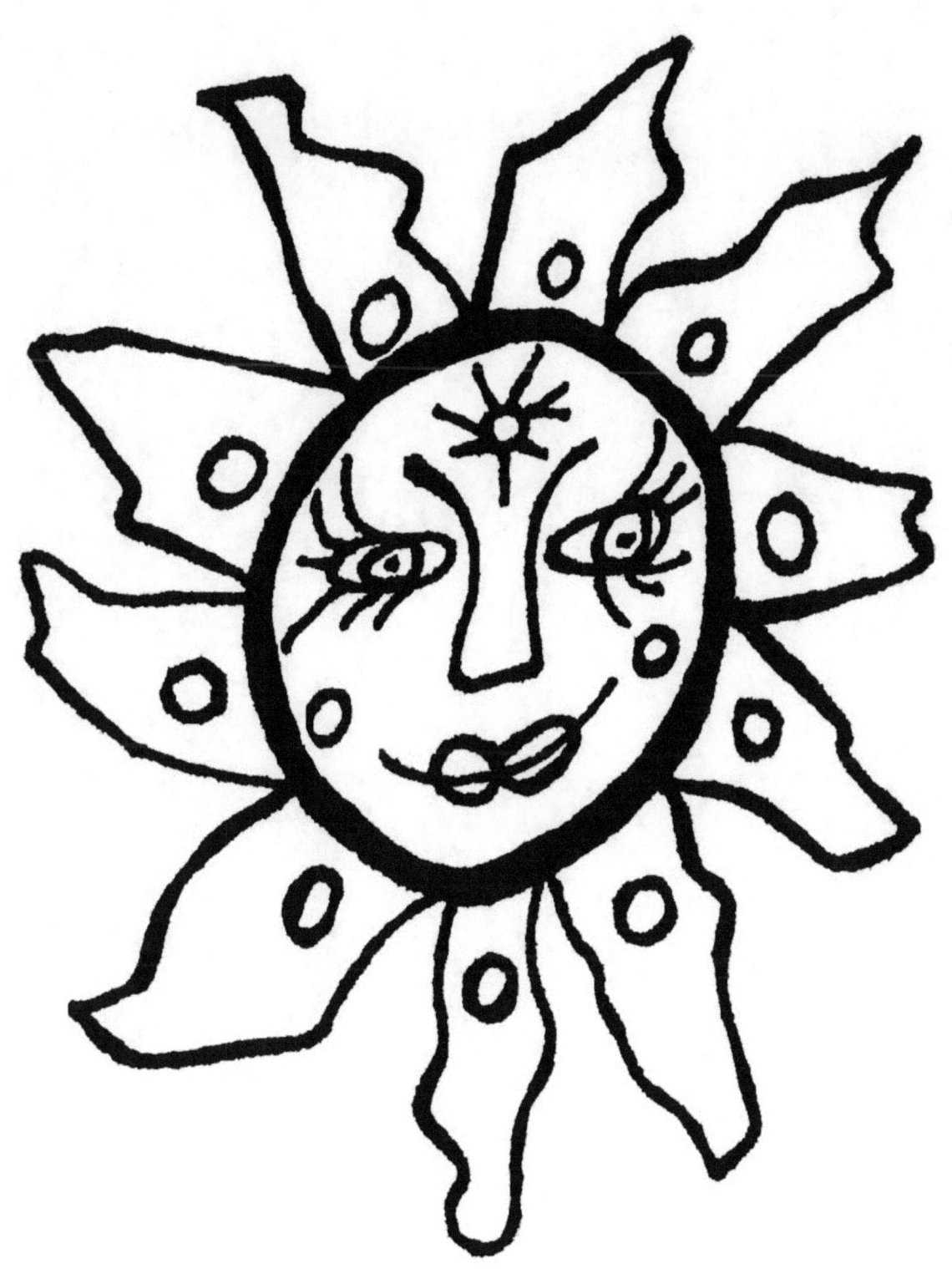

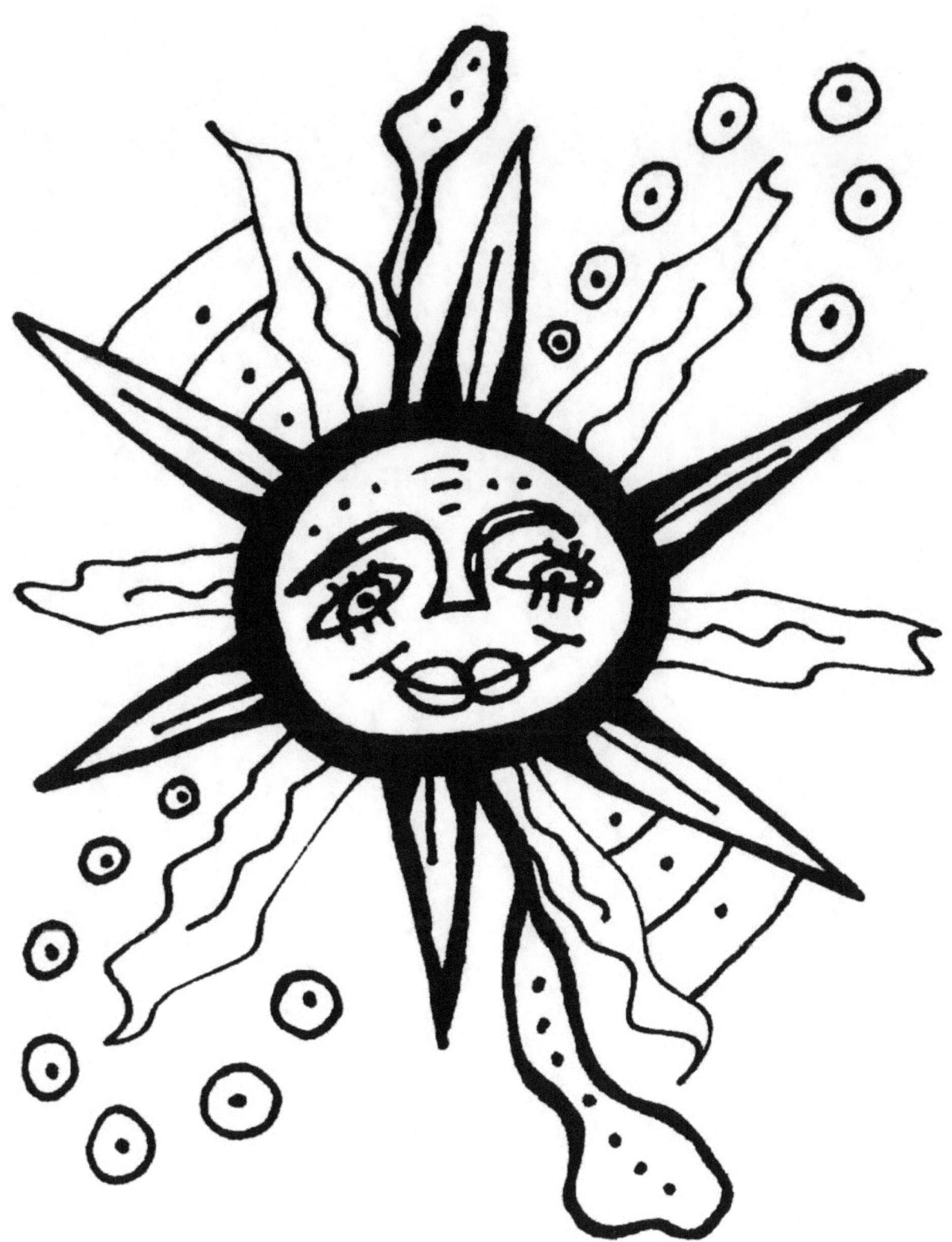

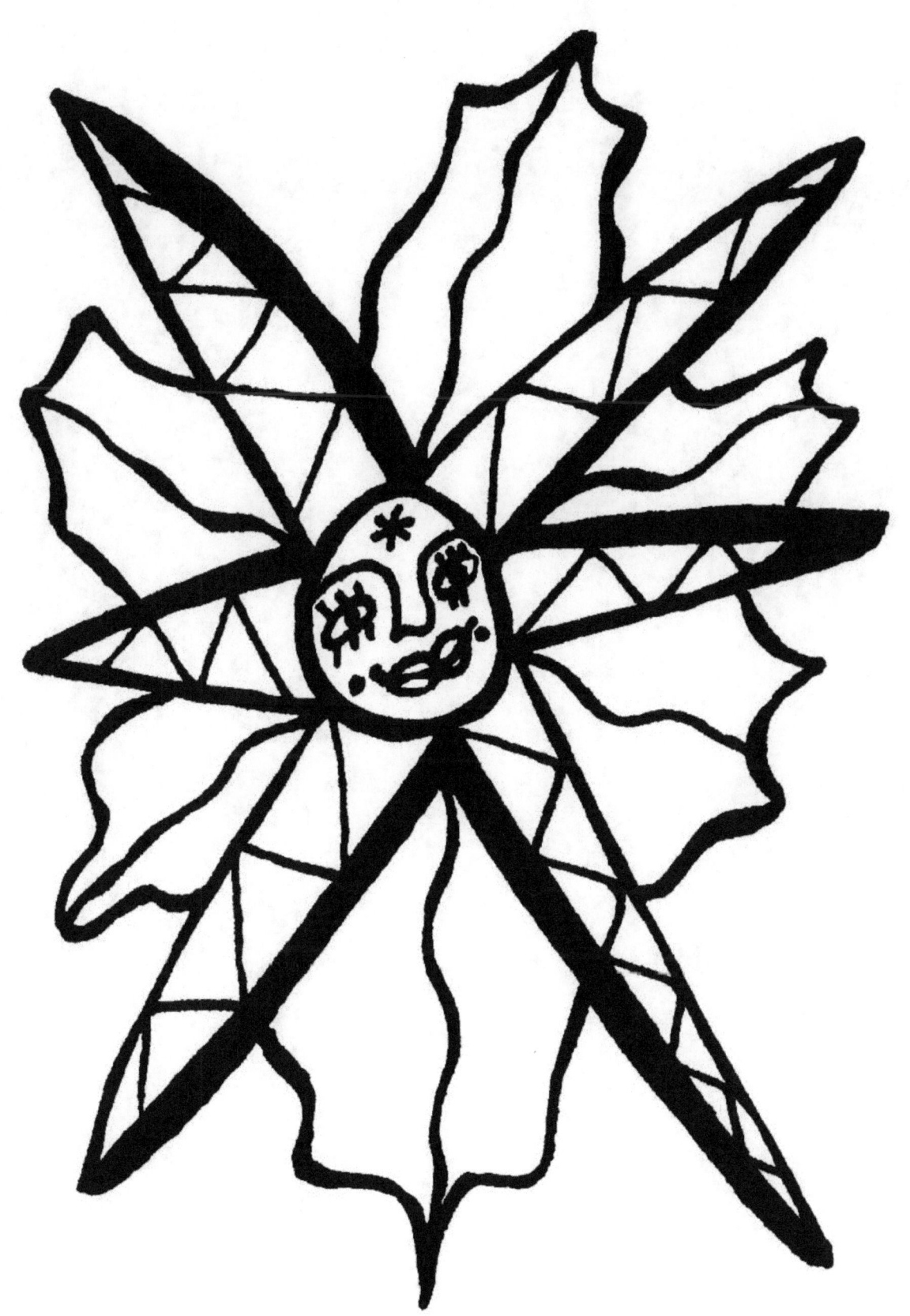

www.ingramcontent.com/pod-product-compliance
Lightning Source LLC
Chambersburg PA
CBHW080606180526
45168CB00007B/2806